"A brainy, brawny, thematically expansive work, stuffed with challenging socio-political ideas and dialectical fireworks . . . Kushner's social engagement and his intellectualism are balanced, as always, by his penetrating humanism."

—DAVID ROONEY, *HOLLYWOOD REPORTER*

"Meaty and brilliant . . . Kushner's dialogue is packed and furious, but it's beautifully constructed. There are nods to several of the great American family plays—*All My Sons*, *A View from the Bridge*—tied up within it, but this is very much a twenty-first-century work which sets out to reflect what has become of us."

—DAISY BOWIE-SELL, *WHATSONSTAGE*

"It is bracing, in an age of mini-dramas, to find a play that throws in everything from Marx to modern materialism . . . The play, which makes constant use of overlapping dialogue to convey family tensions, has a furious energy and deals with the disillusion in an Italian-American community, and by implication a whole society, whose dreams have not been realized. Tony Kushner's turbulent epic fizzes with ideas."

—MICHAEL BILLINGTON, *GUARDIAN*

"You know you're in the hands of Tony Kushner when the characters are wrestling with big ideas in fraught situations, the laughter is plentiful, and you leave feeling smarter than you were before."

—ROBERT HURWITT, *SF GATE*

"Tony Kushner's often blindingly radiant . . . always un-look-away-able megaplay . . . is a play about negation: If *Angels in America* was Kushner's Great Society–size gambit to annex History itself—for the theater, for social justice, for the possibility of Civilizational Upgrade even beyond the bristling self-defense grid welded permanently in place by Reagan—then this is Kushner for the Age of Austerity."

—SCOTT BROWN, *VULTURE*

"Kushner serves up the expected thought-provoking erudition, but it's cut with satisfyingly soapy histrionics and acerbic humor."

—ELISABETH VINCENTELLI, *NEW YORK POST*

"America's most hyperliterate, humorous playwright . . . Tony Kushner has finally gotten around to crafting his own gloriously dysfunctional domestic drama."

—MELISSA ROSE BERNARDO, *ENTERTAINMENT WEEKLY*

"Sprawling, yearning, and at times emotionally violent; it is also packed with a level of complexity, sophistication, and understanding that distinguishes it as an important new American work."

—QUINTON SKINNER, *VARIETY*

THE
INTELLIGENT
HOMOSEXUAL'S GUIDE
TO CAPITALISM
AND SOCIALISM
WITH A KEY
TO THE SCRIPTURES

OTHER BOOKS BY TONY KUSHNER PUBLISHED BY TCG

Angels in America: A Gay Fantasia on National Themes
Part One: Millennium Approaches
Part Two: Perestroika

A Bright Room Called Day

Caroline, or Change

Death & Taxes: Hydriotaphia & Other Plays

A Dybbuk and Other Tales of the Supernatural
(adapted from S. Ansky;
translations by Joachim Neugroschel)

Homebody/Kabul

The Illusion
(adapted from Pierre Corneille)

Lincoln
(the screenplay)

Thinking About the Longstanding Problems of Virtue
and Happiness: Essays, a Play, Two Poems and a Prayer

THE
INTELLIGENT
HOMOSEXUAL'S GUIDE
TO CAPITALISM
AND SOCIALISM
WITH A KEY
TO THE SCRIPTURES

A PLAY BY

Tony Kushner

THEATRE COMMUNICATIONS GROUP
NEW YORK
2023

The Intelligent Homosexual's Guide to Capitalism and Socialism with a Key to the Scriptures is published by Theatre Communications Group, Inc. 520 Eighth Avenue, 20th Floor, Suite 2000, New York, NY 10018-4156

The publication of *The Intelligent Homosexual's Guide to Capitalism and Socialism with a Key to the Scriptures* by Tony Kushner, through TCG Books, is made possible with support by Mellon Foundation.

A number of generous donors have supported this publication. We thank them all at the back of the book.

TCG books are exclusively distributed to the book trade by Consortium Book Sales and Distribution.

Library of Congress Control Numbers:
2017040208 (print) / 2017043941 (ebook)
ISBN: 978-1-55936-489-8 (print) / ISBN: 978-1-55936-8001 (ebook)
A catalog record for this book is available from the Library of Congress.

Book design and composition by Lisa Govan
Cover design by Mark Melnick

First Edition, September 2023

With deep respect for their long, courageous, extraordinary journeys, for their passionate, unyielding commitment to social and economic justice, and with gratitude for their kindness, for their generosity, and most of all, for Oskar—this play is dedicated to Erwin and Doris Marquit. They didn't agree with everything in it, and they told me so, for which I am also grateful.

CONTENTS

THE
INTELLIGENT
HOMOSEXUAL'S GUIDE
TO CAPITALISM
AND SOCIALISM
WITH A KEY
TO THE SCRIPTURES

The play in its current state was developed over the course of four productions. I'm deeply indebted to everyone involved:

The Intelligent Homosexual's Guide to Capitalism and Socialism with a Key to the Scriptures received its world premiere at the Guthrie Theater (Joe Dowling, Artistic Director) in Minneapolis, Minnesota, on May 22, 2009. It was directed by Michael Greif, the set design was by Mark Wendland, the costume design was by Clint Ramos, the lighting design was by Kevin Adams, the sound design was by Ken Travis, the original music was by Michael Friedman; the dramaturg was Jo Holcomb and the stage manager was Martha Kulig. The cast was:

PILL	Stephen Spinella
ELI	Michael Esper
PAUL	Michael Potts
BENNIE*	Kathleen Chalfant
V	Ron Menzel
EMPTY	Linda Emond
GUS	Michael Cristofer
MAEVE	Charity Jones
SOOZE	Mee Chomet
ADAM	Mark Benninghofen
SHELLE	Michelle O'Neill

*The character's name was subsequently changed to Clio.

iHo received its New York premiere in a co-production by The Public Theater (Oskar Eustis, Artistic Director; Joey Parnes, Interim Executive Director) and Signature Theatre Company (James Houghton, Founding Artistic Director; Erika Mallin, Executive Director) on May 5, 2011. It was directed by Michael Greif, the set design was by Mark Wendland, the costume design was by Clint Ramos, the lighting design was by Kevin Adams, the sound design was by Ken Travis, the original music was by Michael Friedman; the production stage manager was Martha Donaldson. The cast was:

PILL	Stephen Spinella
ELI	Michael Esper
PAUL	Todd Freeman
CLIO	Brenda Wehle
V	Steven Pasquale
EMPTY	Linda Emond
GUS	Michael Cristofer
MAEVE	Danielle Skraastad
SOOZE	Hettienne Park
ADAM	Matt Servitto
SHELLE	Molly Price

iHo was produced by Berkeley Repertory Theatre (Tony Taccone, Artistic Director; Susan Medak, Managing Director) on May 21, 2014. It was directed by Tony Taccone, the set design was by Christopher Barecca, the costume design was by Meg Neville, the lighting design was by Alexander V. Nichols, the sound design was by Jake Rodriguez; the stage manager was Michael Suenkel. The cast was:

PILL	Lou Liberatore
ELI	Jordan Geiger
PAUL	Tyrone Mitchell Henderson

CLIO	Randy Danson
V	Joseph J. Parks
EMPTY	Deirdre Lovejoy
GUS	Mark Margolis
MAEVE	Liz Wisan
SOOZE	Tina Chilip
ADAM	Anthony Fusco
SHELLE	Robynn Rodriguez

iHo received its UK premiere at Hampstead Theatre (Edward Hall, Artistic Director; Greg Ripley-Duggan, Executive Director) in London, on October 15, 2016. It was directed by Michael Boyd, the set design was by Tom Piper, the lighting design was by Wolfgang Goebbel, the sound design was by Fergus O'Hare; the stage manager was Michael Dennis. The cast was:

PILL	Richard Clothier
ELI	Luke Newberry
PAUL	Rhashan Stone
CLIO	Sara Kestelman
V	Lex Shrapnel
EMPTY	Tamsin Greig
GUS	David Calder
MAEVE	Sirine Saba
SOOZE	Katie Leung
ADAM	Daniel Flynn
SHELLE	Katy Stephens

CHARACTERS

PILL MARCANTONIO *(PierLuigi = P.L. = Pill)*, 53, Italian-American, high school history teacher, Gus's son

ELI, mid-20s, a hustler

PAUL DAVIS, 47, African-American, formerly an assistant professor of theology at Columbia University/Union Theological Seminary, now a visiting lecturer at the University of Minnesota, Pill's husband

CLIO MARCANTONIO *(sometimes called Zeeko [Zia Clio = Aunt Clio] by her nephews and niece)*, 69, Italian-American, former Discalced Carmelite nun, former Maoist, Gus's sister

V MARCANTONIO *(Vito = Vin, Vic, Vinnie, V)*, 38, Italian-American, building contractor, Gus's son

EMPTY MARCANTONIO *(Maria Teresa = M.T. = Empty)*, 49, Italian-American, formerly a nurse, now a labor lawyer, Gus's daughter

GUS MARCANTONIO, 72, Italian-American, retired longshoreman, lifetime member of the Communist Party USA

MAEVE LUDENS, 40, Doctor of Theology, same-sex partner of Empty

SOOZE MOON MARCANTONIO, early 30s, Korean-American, wife of V

ADAM HERVEY, early 50s, real-estate lawyer, Empty's ex-husband

MICHELLE O'NEILL, 40s, called Shelle, Irish-American

SETTING

The play takes place in Gus Marcantonio's brownstone on Clinton Street, Carroll Gardens, Brooklyn, with side trips to a couple of locations in Manhattan, from Friday–Sunday, June 15–17, 2007.

An Introduction, An Apology, A User's Guide

A Note for Actors and Readers Regarding Dashes, Ellipses, Indents and Overlapping Dialogue

Plays are written to be read. That's their primary purpose, in the sense that reading is the first thing that happens to a play after it's written. Obviously most plays are written ultimately to be performed, but before that, they're read by the people who'll perform them. They'll also be read by people who don't perform, including some who are entirely uninterested in theater, for whom the theatrical life of a play is less meaningful than its life as literature, as something to be read.

A play's theatrical life is intermittent; following every production, the play enters theatrical limbo, where it lingers till its next staging, if there is one. That's why subsequent productions are called revivals—the play's revivified, it's brought back to life. Its continuous, uninterrupted existence is in print, as a book. If a play has longevity, it has its readers, more than its watchers, to thank.

The way a play's dialogue is laid out on the page, the idiosyncratic punctuation playwrights often employ, the thickness or thinness of stage directions: these are clues and signals from the playwright to people who may stage the play, as well as to readers who have no intention of doing so. The playwright hopes these effects will give a reader, sitting alone with a book, an approximation of the electricity and velocity of the play in performance. That imagined performance is not the whole purpose of reading a play. A reader can stop a play's narrative, even reverse it; she can linger, ponder, dig down deep, analyze with control over the forward momentum which holds theater audiences in thrall. A reader has a better chance of understanding certain complex aspects of a play than has an audience member. Even so, any reader of a play is likely to imagine it on its feet, compelled by the oddness, the open-endedness, the severe economies and blank spaces of the dramatic literary form. And the reverse is true: In performance, the paper play haunts its theater audience, troubling the audience's experience of what appears to be a succession of spontaneous events with an awareness that what they're witnessing is spontaneous-yet-not; what unfolds before them is also an elaborate kind of reading-aloud of a printed, fixed text.

This is what I love about reading and watching and writing plays, this ambiguous, amphibious, boundary-crossing quality that's part of theater's unceasing incompleteness, theater's particular dialectical dynamism. I feel that no play is fully realized until it's published, in print, available to readers.

I write this by way of an apology in advance to the readers of this play. It's the only play of mine that wasn't published after its first production. There are a few reasons for this, addressed in the afterword; one cause of the long delay has been a struggle to make the play readerly. I believe it mostly is. But there are passages—in Act One, Scene Two; Act Two, Scene One; and Act Two, Scene Four—during which several people are onstage, speaking at the same time, and even in less densely populated scenes, the characters—a passionate, articulate, but not particularly polite bunch—tend to speak over one another. I've tried various ways to notate these exchanges, finally returning to the method I'd originally employed, which requires placing some lines out of sequence and breaking up others. This presents you, the reader, with the task of deciphering and reassembling. It isn't hard to do (it helps if you enjoy jigsaw puzzles). But the effort required may make these scenes read as effortful, which I believe is not the case when they're performed.

I hope the following guidelines will be useful to you as you read:

When a character's line ends in a dash, the character is stopping abruptly, either because s/he has been interrupted or is interrupting her- or himself.

When a line ends in an ellipsis, the character trails off, leaving something unfinished or unsaid.

When there's an indentation within a speech, it indicates a slight break in the flow of the character's speaking, owing to an internally generated change in subject or tactic.

When a character's line ends with *(cont'd below:)*, find the character's next line; the character's name will be followed by *(cont'd from above)*. This means that the character speaks continuously, with no pause between the end of one line and the beginning of the next. For example, in Act One, Scene One:

PILL

You asked me about . . .
(He stops, upset. He takes a breath.)
Good plays, had I seen good plays in Minneapolis. So, yes— *(cont'd below:)*

ELI

But I— Do you think your dad's seriously—

PILL *(cont'd from above)*
Major Barbara. George Bernard— *(cont'd below:)*

ELI
I know who wrote—

PILL *(cont'd from above)*
—Shaw. It's— I don't go out, much, I'm not supposed to
etc., etc.

Pill says, "Good plays, had I seen good plays in Minneapolis.
So, yes, *Major Barbara.* George Bernard Shaw. It's— I don't
go out, much, I'm not supposed to *etc., etc.*," speaking uninterruptedly. Immediately after Pill says, "So, yes—" Eli says,
"But I— Do you think your dad's seriously—" while Pill keeps
talking, and when Pill says, "George Bernard—" Eli says,
"I know who wrote—" while Pill continues to talk.

The dash following Pill's "George Bernard—" is not indica-
tive of Pill being interrupted, or changing the subject. He'll
go on uninterruptedly to "—Shaw." In such instances, a dash
merely indicates the point at which another character will
begin speaking, rather than an interruption.

When a character's name is followed by *(over above)*, the character starts talking at the end of the line above the line that
immediately precedes his or her line. For example:

GUS *(to Empty)*
What are you all of a sudden a, a neurologist? *(cont'd
below:)*

PILL
It was like 1986 when he died. Wasn't Reagan president?

EMPTY *(over above, to Gus)*
Have you been to a neurologist?

CLIO *(to Empty)*	V *(to Empty)*
No. He won't go.	No.

Empty will say, "Have you been to a neurologist?" immediately after Gus asks her, "What are you all of a sudden, a, a neurologist?" —She'll speak over Pill asking, "It was like 1986 when he died. Wasn't Reagan president?"

When two characters' lines are presented side-by-side, as in the example above, both characters speak at the same time, at the end of the line that precedes their lines. After Empty says, "Have you been to a neurologist?" Clio will say, "No. He won't go," and V will say, "No," simultaneously.

When stretches of dialogue are presented in dual columns, each column is played independently of the other, at its own pace. For example:

EMPTY
But she didn't come. *(cont'd below:)*

PILL *(to Gus)*	EMPTY *(cont'd from above, to Clio)*
What papers?	I'm really sorry, Zeeko, I should've been paying
GUS	more— It's been rough
Mine.	at home.
PILL	CLIO
The . . . strike papers, from the filing cabinets upstairs, the—	How's Maeve doing? She's feeling okay?

GUS	EMPTY
Right, my old crap.	She's enormous, now. Just. Scarily huge.

PILL	V
You told me I could see them! You burned them? You kept saying some day, the papers, the papers from the strike, and and the union and the GAI and I've been asking you since—	Yeah, Sooze was like that, enormous, remember? When she—

GUS	EMPTY
You haven't mentioned them in—	Yeah, wow, V, golly, you must have some kind of super-cum, look at all these gigantic fetuses you make!

PILL	V
That's, that's not true, I—	That's not what I was— Up yours, asshole. Just . . .

GUS *(still to Pill)*

Well I forgot then!

PILL

I've been asking since since since graduate school!

After Empty says, "But she didn't come," Pill asks Gus, "What papers?" while Empty continues with, "I'm really sorry, Zeeko." Pill and Gus argue about the strike papers while Empty, Clio and V talk about Maeve's pregnancy and V's semen. Each of these exchanges should take close to the same time to complete, but adjustments in pace may be necessary to make sure that V has finished saying "Up yours, asshole, just . . ." before Gus interrupts Pill with "Well I forgot then!"

Actors and directors who plan to stage the play, and anyone curious about some of the technical challenges presented by the overlapping dialogue, are encouraged to read the Playwright's Notes that begin on page 273. Or, well, I encourage curious people to read these notes; I *implore* actors and directors to read them!

Two pennies will buy a rose.
Three pennies and who can tell?

—LAURA NYRO, "BUY AND SELL"

ACT ONE

Late afternoon, June 15, 2007, Carroll Gardens, Brooklyn. Pill is standing at the foot of the stoop in front of his father's brownstone, speaking into his cell phone.
Eli's on his cell phone (it's a brand-new iPhone, first-generation!) somewhere in Manhattan.

ELI

So.
Any good theater in Minneapolis?

PILL

When can I see you?

ELI

Ummmm . . . Not tonight.

PILL

You're . . . ?

ELI

Engaged. Otherwise.

PILL

Booked.

ELI

Yep. Yyyyyyep.

PILL

You said you wouldn't, you weren't going to—

ELI

No, I—

PILL

Yes you did, Eli, you said—

ELI

How's your dad?

(Pill looks up quickly at the windows on the parlor floor.)

ELI

I have to get going.

PILL

Please. After you— *(cont'd below:)*

ELI

It'll be really late, I— *(cont'd below:)*

PILL *(cont'd from above)*

Please can I?

18

ELI *(cont'd from above)*

I don't think we should.

PILL

We're going to discuss it.

ELI

Discuss . . . ? *(cont'd below:)*

PILL

His decision, we— *(cont'd below:)*

ELI *(cont'd from above)*

Oh, his— What he wants to do.

PILL *(cont'd from above)*

We're going to talk.
The family.
A family talk.

ELI

Is he actually gonna— Do you think he's serious? About—

PILL

Major Barbara.

ELI

Who?

PILL

You asked me about . . .
(He stops, upset. He takes a breath.)
Good plays, had I seen good plays in Minneapolis. So, yes—
(cont'd below:)

19

ELI

But I— Do you think your dad's seriously—

PILL *(cont'd from above)*

Major Barbara. George Bernard— *(cont'd below:)*

ELI

I know who wrote—

PILL *(cont'd from above)*

—Shaw. It's— I don't go out, much, I'm not supposed to, they want me to curtail my socializing without Paul. And Paul doesn't like, he's *never* liked theater, he's— Film. Sometimes he wants to go to a film, so long as it's you know underlit or over-exposed, so long as there's no pleasure to be derived from it. But we went to see *Major Barbara*, and it was good, you know, Shaw!— *(cont'd below:)*

ELI

Yeah, we read him in Twentieth Century Something-Or-Other.

PILL *(cont'd from above)*

Spinning his contradictions. Dizzying, a head rush, sort of like, sort of like—oh I dunno, poppers, or speed or E or—

(Eli laughs. Pill's pleased at that.)

PILL

Or an infarction. Fun! But then, I don't know, my early train-ing kicks in: It's gradualism! Blech! It's the emasculation of the working class by a sentimental pseudo-socialist, peddling an idealist conception of history!

ELI

Oh yeah, baby, talk commie talk to—

PILL

No, ugh, bleah, I hate it when I—
Some asshole's cell phone went off in the middle of Under-
shaft's big speech in the last act. And the actor, the actor
winced, he lost his focus, he— I, I, you know, thank God I'm
not an actor, at least I was spared *that* indignity, if little else,
but if I was an actor, if I was, I'd hurl myself off the stage at
whatever part of the audience the ringing was coming from and
find the fucking *cyborg* who just couldn't *bear* to turn off his
cell phone and, and stuff the goddamned thing ringing right
down his stupid fucking throat.

(Pause.)

ELI

You sound angry.

(Pause.)

PILL

Do I? I can't imagine why.
I have no words. To tell you how much I—

*(The door of the brownstone opens. Paul steps out. Pill hurriedly
slaps his cell phone shut, hanging up. Too late; Paul's seen it.)*

ELI *(startled)*

Uh . . . You . . . ?
Huh.

*(Eli stares at his cell phone.
Paul and Pill stare at one another, an awkward and ugly
silence.)*

PAUL

Unreal. Un. Real.

(Silence. Pill puts his cell phone in his pocket.
Eli taps two buttons on his iPhone: "call history" and Pill's
number.)

PILL

I just . . .

(Pill's cell phone rings.)

PAUL

Let me talk to him.

(They stand there, Pill's cell phone ringing.
Eli's listening to the rings. Pill's voice mail picks up.)

	PILL'S VOICE MAIL
PAUL	RECORDING
They're waiting upstairs.	Hi, it's Pill. As advertised.
I'm going to Maeve's.	Leave a message. *(beep)*

PILL	ELI
I'll see you . . .	Hey, it's me. Eli. I . . . don't
	know what to tell you to do.

PAUL

Or not.

ELI

I guess I'll be here. Later. I missed you too. A lot.
You do sound angry.

(Eli hangs up.
Pill goes up the stoop as Paul descends.

At the top of the stoop, Pill watches as Paul starts to walk away. Then Paul stops, retraces his steps, and sits on the stoop. He takes a partially smoked cigar from a jacket pocket, and puts it in his mouth.)

PILL

Don't light it.

(Paul, not turning around, flips Pill the bird. Pill goes inside.)

Scene Two

Clio, Empty, V and Gus sit around the dining table that occupies the center of the first floor parlor, which serves as the living/dining room. The kitchen is located behind this room.
Pill hesitates in the vestibule. He takes his cell phone out of his pocket, flips it open, caresses the little glowing screen with his thumb.
Clio calls out:

CLIO

Come on, Pill.

V

Yeah I gotta get home.

(Pill closes the phone. Holding it in his hand, he enters. He keeps the phone in his hand throughout the scene.)

EMPTY *(to Pill)*

Did you see how weedy the garden's gotten?

CLIO *(to Empty)*	PILL *(to Empty)*
Did you notice the barbecue?	I was out front, I didn't—

EMPTY *(to Clio)*

It looks—

GUS

What garden? *(cont'd below:)*

PILL

She means the—

EMPTY *(over the above, to Gus)*

The yard.

GUS *(cont'd from above)*

We never gardened.

EMPTY

Nonno had vegetables out there, he did so.

GUS

Yeah but that was Nonno, *I* never— *(pointing at Clio) She* certainly never grew anything, so what garden are you— 'Cause Nonno died long before you were born.

EMPTY

No he didn't, he—

GUS

He died before the, the—oh fucking hell. *(to Clio)* You *see*?!
I can't remember a goddamned— When did Papa die?

v *(to Gus)*   CLIO
Stop it, you know   You know same as me, Gus.
when he—

GUS *(to Clio)*
Stop testing me! I'm telling you I—

EMPTY *(to Gus)*

Don't shout at—

GUS *(to Empty)*
She's testing me! *(to Clio)* I have Alzheimer's!

EMPTY   CLIO
You don't.   So I hear.

GUS *(to Empty)*
What are you all of a sudden a, a neurologist? *(cont'd below:)*

PILL

It was like 1986 when he died. Wasn't Reagan president?

EMPTY *(over above, to Gus)*
Have you been to a neurologist?

CLIO *(to Empty)*   v *(to Empty)*
No. He won't go.   No.

GUS *(cont'd from above)*
I don't remember when your Nonno my own fucking father—
(to Pill) Not 1986, 1990. He died in 1990.

PILL

Hey look at that,
Alzheimer's cleared right
up. Did you think you were
losing your memory last
year? When you . . .

v *(to Gus)*

You don't have
Alzheimer's.

CLIO

When you slit your wrists?

(Little pause.)

EMPTY

Was that because of the Alzheimer's?

v

Ostensible.

GUS

Incipient. You can't act like a baby now, Vinnie, you tell them— *(to Pill and Empty)* He's been around here, he knows I—

v

What, you mean like that, all those names you couldn't remember, all that old Communist Party shit? *(cont'd below:)*

GUS

The Committees of Correspondence! Right, that, I— *(cont'd below:)*

v *(cont'd from above)*

Who the fuck could remember that? That proves nothing.

GUS *(cont'd from above, to Empty)*

When they walked out of the Cleveland Convention, Angela Davis and, and who else walked out of—

EMPTY

Ummmm . . . Pete Seeger. And . . . Oh jeez Dad that's ten bil-
lion years ago, I have no—

V	PILL *(to Empty)*
You were a longshoreman, never a politician— Who *cares?*	Wasn't Herbert Aptheker—

EMPTY *(to V)*

He cares. He wasn't *only* a longshoreman.

GUS

Gil Green! That's— *(to Pill)* Not Aptheker, they booed him but
he didn't, he'd *never*, maybe his daughter did, the, the—

PILL

Lesbian.

GUS *(to Pill)*	EMPTY
Oh stop.	She'd already left the party before the Cleveland Convention, she, I guess she was still a Marxist, but—
PILL	
What? Stop what?	
GUS	
Stop already with lesbian this and lesbian that.	CLIO
	She wrote an interesting book. About her father.
PILL	
Anyway, you remembered Gil Green.	EMPTY
	I read it, everyone— *(cont'd below:)*

28

V *(to the room)*

I have to get home soon, Sooze has her book group and I gotta read the kids to sleep. Maybe we can continue this over supper or—

EMPTY *(cont'd from above, to Gus)*

And she is a lesbian, by the way, Dad, Bettina, she is a certified card-carrying—

GUS *(over Empty and V above, to Pill)*

Because, because she's there, and you, and you're cueing me, it comes back, with you kids. But over and over, it's just . . . not there. Blank spaces, not like forgetfulness, but. Like *trying to remember* has become this dangerous thing, it . . . pulls *me* into the blank space, I'm . . . *I become the irretrievable, I go away.* *(to Empty)* You were a nurse, is that *normal?*

EMPTY

I wasn't a neurologist.

GUS

It's in the family DNA, Alzheimer's. They just didn't call it that, then, "pazzo," but—

EMPTY

How come if you're losing your memory you're burning all your papers in the barbecue?

PILL	GUS *(to Clio)*
What papers?	You told her? Why?

CLIO *(to Gus)*

It looks like a bomb went off back there, so I called her and said come see what your father's doing.

EMPTY
But she didn't come. *(cont'd below:)*

PILL *(to Gus)*
What papers?

GUS
Mine.

PILL
The . . . strike papers,
from the filing cabinets
upstairs, the—

GUS
Right, my old crap.

PILL
You told me I could see
them! You burned them?
You kept saying some day,
the papers, the papers from
the strike, and and the
union and the GAI and I've
been asking you since—

GUS
You haven't mentioned
them in—

PILL
That's, that's not true, I—

EMPTY *(cont'd from
above, to Clio)*
I'm really sorry, Zeeko,
I should've been paying
more— It's been rough
at home.

CLIO
How's Maeve doing? She's
feeling okay?

EMPTY
She's enormous, now. Just.
Scarily huge.

V
Yeah, Sooze was like that
enormous, remember?
When she—

EMPTY
Yeah, wow, V, golly, you must
have some kind of super-
cum, look at all these
gigantic fetuses you make!

V
That's not what I was— Up
yours, asshole. Just . . .

GUS *(still to Pill)*
Well I forgot then!

PILL

I've been asking since since since graduate school!

GUS

I have Alzheimer's.

PILL

Just to look, to see them for—

GUS

For what?! What's the—

EMPTY

Because he's a historian, Dad, a labor historian.

GUS

He's not a, a, a, *historian*, he's a high school history—

PILL

Oh fuck you Pop

v *(admonishing)*

Come on, Gus.

PILL *(to V)*

What?! I am a high school teacher, I'm not *ashamed* of being a—

v

Fuck you, man, I'm just trying to— *(cont'd below:)*

GUS *(to V)*

Are you mad at me that I called you a baby? *(cont'd below:)*

v *(cont'd from above, to Pill, ignoring Gus)*

I was just trying to stand up for you.

GUS *(cont'd from above, to both Empty and V)*

He's, he's hurt I called you a baby. Vinnie, I didn't—

PILL *(over above, to V)*

Well *don't!* Okay?! It's, I dunno, oh Mr. Butch Contractor, thanks for saving me from the, the old troll of a longshoreman, and oh, and you bring up the kids— *(to Empty)* Have you noticed, I've noticed, every time he *[Gus]* launches into one of his diatribes about lezzies and fags, every—

V *(standing up)*

Fuck this, I'm going back to my excuse-me-for-mentioning-them family including your niece and nephew— *(cont'd below:)*

GUS *(over above, to Pill)*

I said no such thing. I said no such—

V *(cont'd from above, to Pill)*	PILL *(to Gus)*
Your *goddaughter*, you *jerk*. Jesus, what's . . . Nice seeing you again! *(cont'd below:)*	You know perfectly well what you said, *comrade*.

GUS *(to Pill)*

Watch it!

V *(cont'd from above, to Pill)*

God, the pair of you, you . . . She's on me about— And you, you've been a nasty little cunt to me— *(cont'd below:)*

PILL

Oh, a cunt!

v *(cont'd from above, to Empty and Clio)*
Sorry. *(to Pill)* I mean please explain to me what's eating you,
and don't go making a big thing about cunt—dick then, that
better?! What the fuck're you so—

CLIO

He's upset because his father wants to kill himself, Vito.

(V stands there. Little pause.)

CLIO

Your father too by the way.
You think you could sit down now so we can finally talk about
that? You think your wife will miss her book club meeting so
you can stay and talk it over with us? I think she will. You
aren't asking me but that's what I feel you ought to do.

*(Silence.
V looks at Gus, frightened.)*

V

My . . . birthday was last week, so I . . . I guess I thought I dunno
this is just a a whatever, anniversary reaction, to your—to
remembering that she . . .
I mean thirty-eight years is a long time but. Also it isn't.

GUS

I shouldn't've cut my wrists on your birthday. It wasn't— In my
head, it was your mother's, yeah, well, anniversary, because,
it's unfortunate she died on your birthday so . . .

PILL

So you thought you'd give him a matching set.

EMPTY

She died giving birth, anyway, not on his—

GUS

It's the same—

EMPTY

No, I mean you make it sound like she, you know, baked a cake and then toppled over into it.

GUS

So I decided, this time: *after* your birthday. Not *on*. I waited.

EMPTY

So . . .
Are you going to do the open veins in the warm bathtub again?

(Gus doesn't respond, doesn't look at them. Then he shakes his head no.)

v *(quietly, sadly)*

'Cause that . . . That was awful.
And, and really, it like seriously fucked up the, the upstairs bathroom, the . . . the grout.

(Another pause. Empty and Pill look at one another. Empty, losing her effort to suppress a laugh, snorts, which sets Pill off. They laugh. No one else does.)

EMPTY

Sorry, sorry, I . . . never get sleep anymore, I'm . . .

(They stop laughing.)

V

Jesus.

(Empty loses it again, and Pill follows.)

EMPTY

Sorry, sorry . . .

CLIO

You finished?

(They get it under control.)

GUS

She threatened to call the cops and have me committed if
I didn't tell you kids.

CLIO

No such thing, you asked me if I'd called Empty and—

EMPTY *(over above, to Gus)*

We could, Dad, we could put you away.

GUS

For a week maybe. What's it buy you? *(a little pride)* You think
I can't talk my way out of that?

EMPTY *(a little admiration)*

No, you can.

GUS

You bet. One-two—

V

So, huh, so then—

35

(Little pause.)

EMPTY

So Dad?

GUS

What, honey?

EMPTY

If all four of us want you to, to not kill yourself. To face . . . whatever this is, if it's, even if it's Alzheimer's— It's not, I think it's . . .

PILL

Loneliness.

GUS

What?

PILL

Maybe, or . . .

V

Boredom.

EMPTY

Depression, or—

GUS

I'm *not*, and I know you mean well, Pill. But I'm not lonely. And I have never been bored, my *mind*, my mind is *active*, always been that way. I'm already up to the Sixteenth Epistle, Horace, I . . .
(Little pause. Then, from memory:)

"What does the prisoner say to his jailer? If every hope of escape is closed, I can still get out. How? I can die."
That's in the Sixteenth Epistle.

(Gus inhales, aggressively, a huge intake of air, then a huge exhalation, slow and steady.)

EMPTY

I don't know what that . . .
Who's your jailer, Dad?

GUS *(a look at Empty; a beat, then, to her)*

It's complicated.

EMPTY

I'm pretty smart.

GUS

You are. But this . . . *(a shrug)* Complicated, honey.
(little pause)
You remember, I think I told you this, the *Daily News* strike, I helped out, I was ILWU liaison with the Teamsters, the paper and printing trades, when they went out against the *Daily News*? The writers, they went out too, word and muscle, 1991? Same year the Committees of Correspondence broke from the party, same year I left, I left the party, later I rejoined but— *1991*, the year Pop died, and Gorbachev was, you know, that whole . . . *(gesture, something immense)* The coup attempt in Moscow and Yeltsin and Gus Hall, that . . . *(another gesture, throwing away)* The first Iraq—all that crazy shit that year. Anyway. This old guy, this printer, who I met then on the pickets, we liked each other a lot, he was a smart man, he had a perspective, maybe not . . . *(to Clio—she'll know what he means)* But a *perspective*.

CLIO *(she knows what he means)*

Yeah.

GUS

So a year after all that, I got a call that this old printer, the guy's been felled by a heart attack, *wham!* *(he hits himself in the heart, hard)* In a hospital. I went to see him, eyes screwed shut, with a stupid tube down his throat, tape around his mouth to hold it.

I sat for a while, and I noticed his hands was going: *(he shows how the printer's hands were going)* I thought, What is this, like, piano practicing?

(Again with the hands. The gestures aren't much like piano play-ing: the fingers are rapidly moving unseen objects up, down, side-ways.)

Then I thought, Oh I get what—it made me cry, I cried. I thought, his hands want to pull out that tube— Dumb Irish, probably he'd let some cocksucking priest— *(looking at Pill)* Oh, I—

(A quick apologetic gesture to Pill; Pill lets him off the hook.)

GUS

Some creep got to him, talked him out of signing his do-not-resuscitate papers, so . . . And here he was, a prisoner, in that bed. *(he does the printer's hand gestures again)*

His grandson offered me a Kleenex box, and I said, I said look at his hands, he . . . Maybe you think he wants to get at that tube, or the power cord to that goddamn pump? His grandson says, no, that's just muscle memory. He's a typesetter, a com-positor. His hands are still working, see? He's still setting sto-ries and headlines in lead type.

His hands were working. Homo laborans. Homo faber. Man the maker. Man the worker. That's what hands do. The kid was right. But so was I.

(a look at his hands, then) My friend the printer. They left him alone that night, and somehow he dislodged the breathing tube. He asphyxiated.
The work of your hands makes the world. And while you still have the use of them, they can unmake the goddamn world, just as well.

(Little pause.)

EMPTY

I see. *(cont'd below:)*

V

I don't get what's so complicated, it's—

EMPTY *(cont'd from above)*

But I don't— No, I *don't* see. You're not— You're healthy, Dad. You don't have—

V

Can I say one thing.

GUS

Go.

V

Maybe, maybe you need a real job, Daddy.

GUS

I have one. Had. I'm retired, at seventy you're supposed to be retired. I'm seventy-two.

PILL

But you *look*—

39

GUS

Seventy-two.

PILL

But you have great skin.

GUS

Too much of it.

V

You haven't worked since 1973.

GUS

I was a longshoreman for fifty-four years, I only retired in 2005. Mandatory by contract. But for before that I—

V

Yeah, but you only *worked*, I mean lifted cargo, or worked a fork-lift for, what? Thirty-two, thirty-three years tops, before you guys got the Guaranteed Annual Income. *(heading into dangerous territory)* After which you never worked again, you—

EMPTY *(to V)*

Are you kidding? Organizing, that's not work? You should try it. *(cont'd below:)*

V

For money, I mean work for—

GUS *(over above, to Empty)*

It's okay, he—

EMPTY *(cont'd from above, to V)*

He's proud of the GAI. *(to Gus)* It won't kill him to say, "You don't get it."

(V clams up.)

PILL *(to V)*

Don't clam up.

Say on, say— *(to Gus)* He was going to say, and not to disrespect all that you won in '73, in the strike, the, the paper record of which you've *burned*, but, the Guaranteed Annual Income, on which we, which we all owe so much to, I mean your work-free wages, they bought our groceries, well not mine, I was gone, basically, and not Aunt Clio's—

CLIO

I pay for my own groceries.

PILL

You were . . . God alone knows. With the Maoists in Peru—

CLIO

Not till '86.

PILL

—where there aren't any groceries.

GUS

That's not the point, that was never the point of the struggle, a Guaranteed Income isn't about, about groceries, it's—

EMPTY

Actually it *is* about groceries, isn't it? It's—

GUS

Yes, okay, sure, but so, so much more than that, you always wanna tame the, the—

EMPTY

Taming, yeah, well, that's me, right? *(cont'd below:)*

41

GUS

Well isn't it? Take it slow, make it safe for—

EMPTY *(cont'd from above)*

Domesticating the revolution since—

PILL

Okayokayokay but *anyway*, I think what V is saying is . . . V?

V *(to Gus)*

It's just *wrong*. Don't die because you're bored.

GUS

I'm not!

V

You're so bored you learned *Latin*!

EMPTY *(to V)*

Don't provoke him, that's not—

V *(to Empty)*

I'm not! And you *asked* me to be the sperm donor, so why're you being such a— *(cont'd below:)*

EMPTY

Oh V this isn't about that— *(cont'd below:)*

GUS *(over the above, to V)*

Can we please *not* go into that? Please?

V *(cont'd from above, to Empty)*

You been ragging on me since the first I . . . *(quick jerk-off gesture)*

EMPTY *(cont'd from above)*

And anyway Maeve asked you, *I* didn't. *(to Gus)* I *completely* agree. *(gesture to V) BLECH! GROSS! (then to Gus)* You never go to Party meetings, because—

GUS

Because—

EMPTY

Because they're so dead.

V

And you aren't. The Corresponding Whatnot Council and Herbert Ap-whatever, you don't *actually* care about all that, you just think you're supposed to—

GUS *(to Empty)*

I never said that they were dead! They aren't, you haven't been since you were a kid! *(cont'd below:)*

EMPTY

Right! And wild horses couldn't drag me to—

GUS *(cont'd from above)*

The Party isn't dead! Christ! Show some fucking respect for the—

EMPTY

Okay, okay, sure, I mean I'm sure there are good people doing good hard work. But not you. It's been years since you did any fieldwork, organized any drives, any—

(Gus waves this away, impatient.)

EMPTY

But stopping, it's— It's not a capital crime.

V

Man the maker, whyn't you come help me?

GUS

What, you mean . . . ?

V

Come work for me. Let me pay you sub-minimum off the books like I do Sooze's cousins—and promise me you won't organize them. Come help me install lacquered zebrawood cabinets in the kitchens of the soon-to-be-swept-away Brooklyn Heights bourgeoisie.

EMPTY

V will let you write secret messages on their walls.

V

You bet. "Capitalism sucks!" or whatever.

EMPTY

"The money for this twenty-three-year-old hedge fund junior manager's kitchen renovation came from unpaid wages disguised as profit."

PILL

"Capital is dead labor that vampire-like only lives by sucking living labor and lives the more the more labor it sucks." *Kapital*, Volume One, Chapter Ten, "The Working Day."

EMPTY *(impressed)*

High five!

(They high-five each other.)

V

Then we can paper 'em over with sunset ivory watermarked Thai silk wall covering, three hundred and seventy-seven bucks a square foot.

PILL *(to Gus)*

You could, you . . . Maybe you just need some, you know, air.

(Little pause.)

EMPTY

"Productive life is species-life. It is life-producing life." You could write that too.

(Gus looks at her, then at all of them, then back to Empty.)

GUS

Okay, here's the thing. *(looking mostly at V)* I want you all to stay calm. I am, I'm calm. I don't want to make you sad. But I'm your father, I'm going to make you sad, some day, I'll go, eventually, so . . .

Look, the, the house. This brownstone, this is the inheritance, right, the family's wealth, three, four generations of toil and . . . *(gestures to the room, the building)* Ours. We own it. *(pointing to Clio)* She don't want it, she wants . . . *(to Clio)* I don't know what you want.

CLIO *(hands up, as in "Not a thing.")*

I'm good.

GUS

I want to, to—
(a quick glance at V, getting nervous)
The market's softening. Right? We all read the fucking *Times*. We're past the top of the market unless you believe monetarist crap about infinite expansion, unless you have Alzheimer's

45

worse than mine and can't remember . . . 1992, or the '70s, how fast it all comes undone, and, and *this*, what's coming? It's gonna be so much worse than— Barbarism is what we used to call it, money stripping off the human-looking mask, fascism, even. People used to use words like that before everyone got so scared of being scared, because—

PILL *(suspicious)*

Where is this going?

v *(suspicious)*

"The market's softening."
You mean the, the stock market?

GUS

No, not the stock market, who cares about that? The, the—

v *(a quiet threat, a dare)*

The housing market.

GUS

I'm smart enough at least to understand one thing. Okay, two: Boom. Bust. What it's worth today won't be there tomorrow, and—

v

It's a temporary slump. People shouldn't panic.

GUS

Who says so?

v

The Federal Reserve.

GUS

You listen to what the—

V

Yes. I do.

GUS

A little advice: Don't.

Okay so. Hear what I'm saying objectively. Times change and we change with them. Expectations have to yield to, to material realities.

I want to liquidate.

And then vacate.

(Little pause.)

EMPTY

You want to kill yourself and sell the house.

GUS

Sorta. Yeah. Other way around.

PILL

Or: How about you sell, and then, instead of killing yourself, you could, you know, move?

GUS

Yeah. I don't want to.

PILL

A little studio apartment?

GUS

I was born in this house. Clio too. This was the first place you three came home to. I don't want to live elsewhere. I can't.

CLIO

You always could.

47

GUS *(to Clio)*
You could, you do, that's you, I can't, I . . . choose not to.

EMPTY
No, you choose death instead! *Do you hear yourself?*

GUS *(to Empty)*
I choose *not to.* That's a choice, also. Refusal. Flat-out. You don't care for that— *(cont'd below:)*

EMPTY
Fuck me. Is Adam . . . *(cont'd below:)*

GUS *(cont'd from above)*
—you never want to accept that but that's—

EMPTY *(cont'd from above)*
Adam's helping you find a—

GUS
He found one.
It's, um, a lot of money. It's *(embarrassed to be smiling)* four million.
(to V) Way above, above market, so, so if, so if—

(He stops because V is glaring at him. He glares back. V looks away.)

EMPTY
Are you at contract?

(Gus turns from V, to Pill:)

GUS

I don't know what's going on with you, why you guys suddenly moved to Minneapolis, why you look so . . . like the furies are after you all the time, drugs, booze, I don't know, but Jesus, anyone can see you're in need, and, and Paul will know how this can help, and— *(to Empty)* What does a labor lawyer make? Okay I wish the baby was Adam's, at least his, you know, genetic materials, his and yours, not *(to V)* your, your . . . *(repeats the jerk-off gesture)* But I know she's important to you and when I let myself I like her and I know she'd like to be comfortably off— You too, you want comfort too, you didn't used to care, but—

EMPTY

Dad, please stop talking. Just for a—

GUS

Even after taxes, half a million each. Even in this world, it's— Well it's the most you can get. I want you to have the most you can get. And I don't want to leave you, to, to fight over the—

EMPTY

Fight? Who's going to fight over—

(Paul opens the door and enters the room.)

PAUL

May I—
Why am I asking?
(to Pill, calm, with difficulty) You weren't going to participate in this. Correct? You kvetched all the way from the Twin Cities airport to Newark to Morningside Heights, appropriately, I thought, showing some slender benefit derived from all the admittedly less-pricey-than-Manhattan but since *I've* been

paying for it pricey-enough Minneapolitan psychotherapy. All apparently shot to hopeless *shit* by an hour back in this city and the mere prospect of facing these dear people— *(to the others)* You know I love you all, but, but this . . . *conference* or, or gathering of the coven, it legitimizes whatever there is in him of genuine serious suicidal ideation, it wouldn't be a, a good idea probably for most families, but also the man. Is. A. Communist. Party. Member. Cadres. Party discipline, what do I know? *(to Gus)* Gus I love you and Jesus loves you but— *(cont'd below:)*

PILL *(to Gus)*
Don't freak out, he doesn't even believe in Jesus, he's speaking in a manner of speaking, Jesus as signifier.

GUS *(to Pill)*
He's a— *(to Paul)* You're a professor of theology, how can you teach all that stuff and *not* believe in Jesus?

PAUL *(cont'd from above, to Gus)*
—BUT you've spent your whole life in fealty to a veritable machine for the manufacturing of paranoically implosive personalities, the sheer . . . suction of it is staggering. Even sister Clio here, you, we've, how many times have we met?

CLIO
Rarely. Always a pleasure.

PAUL
You tried as I understand it to get away from the whole grim obsessive secretive cult/culture, your father I imagine, Gus.

CLIO
I was a nun and then a Maoist, Paul. I'm comfortable in cults, the grimmer and more obsessive the better.

PAUL

Right, and so the prodigal returns, guarding him since last June!
How's that worked out? *(to the siblings)* And now, what, you're
each going to take your turn? *(to Empty)* You up next, Em?

EMPTY

I have no intention of—

PAUL

You sure you don't? You *intended* to become a doctor. Are you
a doctor? No, because you decided doctors are management.
(cont'd below:)

EMPTY

They *are* management, Paul, doctors. I didn't make that up.

PAUL *(cont'd from above)*

So you became a nurse instead, or that's what you *intended*—
(cont'd below:)

EMPTY

I was a nurse! Fuck you, I was a really good—

PAUL *(cont'd from above)*

—but you became a nurse who organizes other nurses, and
then a labor lawyer— *(cont'd below:)*

EMPTY

Yeah, okay, but—

PAUL *(cont'd from above)*

—and you can tell yourself you *intended* that all along but that
was him, that whole time, his big ole cargo hook sunk in your
soul, pulling you back, and now: Here you are, Em, fucked-up
in fucking Brooklyn again— *(cont'd below:)*

51

EMPTY

I stayed away for a whole year, Paul! You want me to be a, a shitty undutiful daughter, I already got that covered.

PAUL *(cont'd from above)*

—because a year ago he talked you into getting him out of the hospital— *(cont'd below:)*

EMPTY

I couldn't *leave* him there, in that terrible place, he wasn't getting better, he—

PAUL *(cont'd from above)*

—against common sense, his own best interests and the advice of his doctors, you just— *(cont'd below:)*

EMPTY

Oh, seriously? His *doctors*? They were like high school sophomores, they could barely form words! Please.

PAUL *(cont'd from above)*

Break this the fuck up. Call the motherfucking cops. Sit on the manipulative motherfucker till they get here, because none of you have the least idea how far he'll take the need to fuck with your stupid heads. Then get him on a locked ward and fill him full of psychotropics because YOU CAN'T SAVE HIM, NONE OF YOU. You think he's calling out for help but he hasn't, he called *you*, you are in his head and he wants his head to die, what he wants to kill is you.
Oh why am I . . .

PILL

Come on, booboo, let's go for some—

PAUL *(turning suddenly on Pill)*

Look at you, clinging to that phone like it was your hope for eternal salvation. But it isn't, Pill, it's just a carcinogenic little microwave bundled with silicon and arsenic and tantalite from the Congo the mining rights for which millions upon millions of innocents have been slaughtered, that's the Devil in your hand, *you heartless evil wicked faggot*. I've been sitting out on that stoop thinking just try to get past me, just try to go back to him I'll kill you first I'll drag you by your hair to—

Do you *know* what I have done for— Do I *exist*? You have made me doubt it. Not for you, not exist for you, but, but *do I exist*? You have finally dragged me to the Doorstep of Goddamned Despair. And that is NOT in a manner of speaking.

Gus, I sincerely hope you don't kill yourself. You're not half bad. Your son . . . *(to Pill)* Fucking hell.

(Paul leaves.
V is looking at the floor, Clio at the tabletop, Gus and Empty look at Pill, immobile.)

CLIO *(to Pill)*

Should you . . . ?

(V stands up, abruptly.)

V

He had a good idea.
(He walks toward the door.)
I oughta call the cops.

GUS

Please don't, Vin.

V

Don't worry, I'd only do that if I gave a fuck.
You promised me.

(V grabs a bust of Giuseppe Garibaldi from a shelf and punches it headfirst into the wall. He leaves, fast.
Gus is frozen for a moment, then runs after him.
Clio, Empty and Pill look at one another.
Empty goes to the hole V's made in the wall, the base of the bust of Garibaldi sticking out. Carefully she extricates Garibaldi, sets him down, then looks briefly inside the wall. She turns back to Clio and Pill. She gestures "What was that all about?")

CLIO

I think he thought it was his.

EMPTY

The house?

PILL

Why would he— Did Pop
promise him the . . . ?

CLIO

No idea.

EMPTY *(over above, to Pill)*

Oh let him have it.

PILL

He can have your third, he can't have—

(Empty shoots him a look, worried, appalled; then, to Clio:)

EMPTY

Did you know he'd decided to sell the house? *(cont'd below:)*

PILL

Five hundred thousand dollars.

EMPTY *(cont'd from above, to Clio)*

Before he . . . ?

CLIO

Nope.

EMPTY *(a little exasperation)*

I thought, you've been here all year, I thought you'd have talked about—

PILL *(to Empty)*

Five hundred and thirty thousand for you.

EMPTY *(ignoring him, to Clio)*

Do you think his speech is strange?

CLIO

I think all speech is strange.

EMPTY

Should he be . . . just out, running about, shouldn't we— Paul's right, right? We should call the—

CLIO

You should do what you want, call 911 if you want. I have problems with that, but they're mine.

EMPTY

Yeah but you know feel free to *share*.

CLIO

When they arrive, the cops, you're face-to-face with . . . force, a strength way beyond yours, uninterested in specifics of your situation which may be precious to you and extremely significant but to this force have no meaning whatsoever. Gus in a state hospital, filled with drugs that make him incoherent? That's what that'll be. I have a problem with that.

(Pause. Empty nods, considering.)

PILL

I think I've destroyed my marriage.

EMPTY *(to Pill)*

Like my biggest concern is getting paid back.

PILL

I didn't say it was.

EMPTY

We've probably both destroyed our—
Except of course I can't leave mine, or let her just, you know, scream at me and stalk out, because she's about to give birth to my nephew.

(Empty grabs her hair and screams, silently, rocking back and forth. Pill does the same. They both rock and silently scream. When they finish:)

CLIO

Vito's here all the time, fixing stuff. Who'd you think took care of the charnel house that bathroom was, last June, after? He stripped and repainted the walls, put in that beautiful new tub, and he paid for it too. I think he's paid a lot, over the years, to keep the roof from falling in. He sold the old tub for fifteen bucks to Mrs. Dallarizza down the block. Her grandson sawed it in half and made his nonna a shrine for the Virgin. *(she makes the Sign of the Cross)*

EMPTY

I didn't know you— *(vague gesture of making a cross)* You don't still believe that stuff, why do you—

CLIO

Never learned to stop.

EMPTY

Do you know what he plans to . . .
How he plans to do it.

CLIO

He's met someone.

EMPTY

Who?

CLIO

A woman.

PILL

He's . . . ?

EMPTY

Dating? Someone?

CLIO

Michelle. I don't know what goes on. She's your age.

EMPTY

Gross.

PILL

So? He's still hot.

EMPTY

Gross.

PILL

I'd do him.

CLIO

She's helped someone else. I gather she's supplying him the
how-to. Painless.

EMPTY

Huh.

CLIO

Contrary to what Seneca and Cato and the Stoics promised,
I suspect it *hurt*, cutting his wrists, it hurt a lot. And it felt bad
while he was bleeding.

EMPTY

He told you this.

(Clio shrugs.)

EMPTY *(a beat; then)*

Has he asked you to be with him?

(Clio shakes her head no.)

EMPTY

So . . . Michelle? Is her . . . *(name)*?
She'll be with him.

CLIO

Someone will. One thing about Gus: He don't really do anything alone.

(Empty starts to cry.)

PILL

Oh Empty . . .

(She looks up at him, and begins to cry harder.)

EMPTY

Oh Pill . . .

(He goes to her. They embrace. They hold one another.)

CLIO

When you're done crying, you'll need to think. About what you're going to—

(Gus comes through the front door. Empty pulls herself together. Gus enters the parlor. He goes to the hole in the wall. He puts his hand in and cracks off a piece of wallboard, making the hole bigger.)

CLIO

How's V?

(Gus looks at Empty.)

CLIO

You surprised him.

GUS

Yeah.
He took a swing at me.

(He puts the piece of wallboard down on the table, dusts off his hands, and pats Empty's face.)

GUS

I'm going up. I'm tired.

59

EMPTY

Is Adam home?

GUS

I saw his light.
(realizing his plan's endangered) Don't tell him! He doesn't
know I— What I was thinking.

EMPTY

Did he *ask?*

GUS

Don't queer the deal, it's none of your—

EMPTY

You're going to kill yourself in anticipation of a dip in the
housing market, and my ex-husband's your broker. I think that
qualifies as my—

PILL

I'm going out for a minute.

EMPTY

Can you stay? And, you know, *help* with the—

PILL

A minute, Jesus! I have to, to—
(to Gus) And it's not because you said queer. *(to Empty)* I'll be
back in . . .

(Pill leaves.)

EMPTY *(to Gus)*

We'll solve this.
(indicating downstairs) I'm just going to—
(to Clio) I'm sorry, Zeeko. That I left you alone to . . .

CLIO

But now. Now you're here.

EMPTY *(to Gus)*

Promise me you won't— Tonight, you won't—

(He waves her off, annoyed. She kisses him on the cheek.)

EMPTY

I'll just be downstairs.

(Empty leaves.
Gus returns to the hole in the wall, staring at it. Then:)

CLIO

You told *me* to call them, that was your idea.

GUS

Was it? Maybe? I forget.

CLIO

Bullshit.
I can't carry your suicide as my personal splinter of the cross.
I can't stay for this.

GUS

Who's asking you to?
(moving toward his desk) I got work to do before I hit the sack.
I'm tired.

CLIO

You want coffee, or . . .

GUS

Don't be sad, kiddo.

CLIO

Oh Augusto. Sad? That's . . . *(nothing, life)*
The kids, you chose that. *They're* your ultimate. Nothing can matter more.
That's not sentiment. It's hard fact. On Claudia's memory, please.
(little pause)
I know you say you can't but if you said you could. Try. Try to find some other way.

GUS

That's you, Clio. I always admired that. Me, change *that* much, change the way? How'm I gonna pretend that's not surrender? How'd I pretend I believe it's still *me*. That's suicide too.

(Clio looks at him; then she nods. She heads toward the kitchen; Gus watches her go. Clio stops at the framed photo of Vito Marcantonio, and turns back to Gus.)

CLIO

Congressman Marc, egli sta girando nella sua tomba.

GUS

È morto. *(cont'd below:)*

CLIO

Aveva fiducia in te. Il tuo coraggio. La tua forza. *(cont'd below:)*

GUS *(cont'd from above)*

Ciò che i morti pensano non importa.

CLIO *(cont'd from above)*

Credo se sarebbe scontento di voi ora.

(He goes to her, he kisses her tenderly on the lips.)

GUS

Through that face, all of a sudden, you at fifteen comes through.

(He sits at his desk, switches on a table light, opens his Cassell's Latin Dictionary, takes up his small, red-jacketed Loeb Classics Library edition of Horace's Epistles in his left hand, opens it, takes up a pencil in his right, and begins writing in his notebook, translating. Clio watches him. Then:)

CLIO

Now that she's back, I can go.

(Gus doesn't look up. He keeps working.)

Scene Three

In the garden apartment, one floor below the parlor, about five feet below street level, as is evident by the way the street lights light the upper halves of the windows' translucent blinds. Empty and Adam are on the floor, semi- or entirely naked, clothes scattered all about.

EMPTY

If he sells you'll have to relocate. *(cont'd below:)*

ADAM

The new owner might want to keep me, good tenants are—

EMPTY *(cont'd from above)*

Maybe *that's* why you're helping him. Unconsciously, which is how you do everything, you're evicting yourself. *(cont'd below:)*

ADAM

He needed a broker; I'm a broker.

EMPTY *(cont'd from above)*

Maybe you're finally realizing how perverted this is, living in the basement—

ADAM

Garden apartment.

EMPTY

Basement of my father's house. You're a successful real-estate lawyer. We got divorced *five years ago*, Adam. Move out!

ADAM

You're a "successful" labor lawyer which is the same thing as an unsuccessful any-other-kind-of lawyer and yet you get to live in a fucking *two-bedroom co-op* on Riverside Drive— *(cont'd below:)*

EMPTY

It's on 97th Street, not Riverside— You lie for a living.   ·

ADAM *(cont'd from above)*

—which you could *never never've* afforded without your lipsticked gorgon of a divorce lawyer's—

EMPTY

She thoroughly kicked your ass! Who represents *himself* in a— Maybe you're finally realizing you don't belong here.

ADAM

I belong here. Okay? It's my family too. Fuck you, it is. Maybe you're finally realizing you're not a lesbian.

EMPTY

Because of *this*? This is just, this is just meaningless— I love tits, Adam— *(cont'd below:)*

ADAM

You seem— Thanks, by the way—you seem to like it well enough, you were— *(cont'd below:)*

EMPTY *(cont'd from above)*

—just everything about tits. And eating pussy, I *always* loved it, the— *(cont'd below:)*

ADAM *(cont'd from above)*

—you were, you were like, *mooing*, you were—

EMPTY

—you know, the depths, the interiority, the infolded complexities. *Mooing?* Fuck you.

ADAM

Gertrude Stein mooed! When Alice ate her out! *(cont'd below:)*

EMPTY

Gertrude mooed, I moo too, Gertrude was a dyke, ergo— *(cont'd below:)*

ADAM *(cont'd from above)*

Janet Malcolm says so, in the *New Yorker*!

EMPTY *(cont'd from above)*

And it was the other way around, it was Stein who ate out Toklas, you— *(cont'd below:)*

ADAM

And you didn't *always*. You certainly aren't, um, *disinterested* in cocks, as you demonstrated so rambunctiously and clamorously not five minutes ago.

EMPTY *(cont'd from above)*

Alice was a classic bossy bottom, she— You never got how any of that works. You have no imagination, that's your problem, you're— *Un*interested is what you mean, and cocks are, well, in and of themselves, blunt; they only get interesting when they're made of black rubber strapped to a woman, that's more sort of . . . antinomical, at least, not just dull you know *force*, it's— Maeve is too spherical now to strap ours on, any of them, we have a collection. She likes to shop, as foreplay. Or, or she did, none of 'em fit her, now, they don't make maternity strap-ons and anyway anyway being fucked by an eight-months-pregnant dyke wearing a dildo, and you'd have to do it doggy style, it's too much.

ADAM

Wanna go again? Play-acting! *(cont'd below:)*

EMPTY

Adam. *(cont'd below:)*

ADAM *(cont'd from above)*

You're the boy, I'm the girl— *(cont'd below:)*

EMPTY *(cont'd from above)*

Adam. *(cont'd below:)*

ADAM *(cont'd from above)*

—you can use your fingers to—

EMPTY

Blow the deal.

ADAM

The . . . ?

> EMPTY

Please.

> ADAM

It'll do Gus good, to be— *(cont'd below:)*

> EMPTY

No it—

> ADAM *(cont'd from above)*

—to be freed from the considerable expense of maintaining this—

> EMPTY

It won't do him *good*, it will finish him. The house, it's— They died here. They *died here*, Adam: Nicolao, Bisnonna Maria, my grampa Matt, Nonna Rosa. If he feels he's losing his memory— He had a . . . practically an eidetic memory, instant recall of the name of every worker he ever met, and back when he was organizing, strikes, union drives, he met thousands, their kids, spouses. If his whole remembered life is really, um, dissolving. This place— *(looking around, up; then)* It's history. *Our* history. It remembers for him. You really don't belong if you can't understand that.

> ADAM

I'd never want to hurt Gus, you know that. I had no idea that he—

> EMPTY

Scare off the buyer— *(cont'd below:)*

> ADAM

They don't scare easily.

> EMPTY *(cont'd from above)*

—tell them lousy plumbing, termites, mold.

ADAM *(cont'd from above)*

And it's not my decision, it's Gus's.

EMPTY

What're you worried about, your commission?

ADAM

I'm not taking a commission! And may I point out that I've *been* here, with Clio and V! Where's Pill been? Where is he now? And where have *you* been? *(cont'd below:)*

EMPTY

It's been tough, to, to— *(cont'd below:)*

ADAM *(cont'd from above)*

For months you haven't even—

EMPTY *(cont'd from above)*

Work's gotten just, um, exhausting, and, and—

ADAM

Work, oh right, work, *that* justifies abandoning your father after a serious suicide attempt, but I'm an asshole because I found him a four-million—

EMPTY

We're working on EFCA—the Employee Free Choice—

ADAM

I know what EFCA—

EMPTY

Yeah, you're probably against it. *(cont'd below:)*

ADAM

Agnostic, won't impact residential real estate.

EMPTY *(cont'd from above)*

For the Senate debate, we're one of the groups feeding Ted Kennedy's office, we're just a small part of the— But stats, stories, testimony, depositions, I'm on the subway all day every day, restaurant and hotel and some domestic workers—chicken pluckers! In Queens! My Spanish is really, it's totalmente increíble cómo es fluido soy. It's not the Wagner Act, it should be the Wagner Act, but you know it's, after all this . . . *(gestures, then)* Horror. They're going to filibuster it, those greedy dishonest fucks, but next year, if a Democrat gets the White House, it'll be— Well we'll see what it'll be, but it'll be better than what we have now: the worst, the motherfucking unshielded worst. Better and better, I think, if we work for it, and I'm . . . *working.* Harder than I have ever worked before, and I love what I do, working hard on a big-ass federal labor law.

ADAM

God, you are so doomed and beautiful.

EMPTY

My personal life, viewed objectively, everything other than work, it's an awe-inspiring disaster: the whole . . . rat king, and—

ADAM

What's a rat king?

EMPTY

It's . . . irrelevant, it doesn't— Pill got into trouble, and— Forget it. It's mythological. All the rats' tails tangle together and they make a, a, collectively, a new rat. A super rat. The Rat King. So snarled and, and omnidirectionally many-headed it can't move, and it . . . dies.

(a beat; then, confidingly) Maeve's so huge she looks like she's about to, to explode. Or, or float away . . .
(whisper) Adam. Nobody anywhere wants a baby less than I.

ADAM

I know. You should've stayed with me. I'm sterile.

EMPTY

No you're—

ADAM

Low, low motility.

EMPTY

And you make me moo.

ADAM

Okay, here's what you do: tell Gus that it's financially advisable to put off suicide till 2010, when Bush's tax cuts reduce the estate tax to zero. You, Pill and V will walk away with 1.3 million each, tax-free! *(cont'd below:)*

EMPTY

Grow the fuck up, Adam, really, really just—

ADAM *(cont'd from above)*

No no seriously, convince him! He should sell now, then wait three more years to kill himself! By then, if he really has Alzheimer's he might forget that he meant to.

EMPTY

He's not a joke! *My father isn't a—*

ADAM

He wants attention.

71

> **EMPTY**
>
> You don't know what you're talking about. *Attention?* He's the most private man you'll ever— *(cont'd below:)*

> **ADAM**
>
> *Your* attention. *(cont'd below:)*

> **EMPTY** *(cont'd from above)*
>
> He was trained to *avoid*—

> **ADAM** *(cont'd from above)*
>
> He wants that more than anything else on earth.

> **EMPTY** *(thinking about this, then)*
>
> Not more than anything, that's where you're wrong. You've never been able to understand that, I tried for years to explain it, but people like you can't—

> **ADAM**
>
> He wants things to improve, sure, everyone wants that, but—

> **EMPTY**
>
> Not to *improve*. He's a communist. He wants things to *change*. There's an entire *science*, or well at least rigorous structured thought behind what he— If you'd read just one of the books I gave you—*Marx for Beginners*, a fucking *comic book* but even that was too—

> **ADAM**
>
> But that's general, all that political stuff. He misses you. He wants you to be his daughter. Just like any other dad. I'm talking about his, you know, heart. You're *afraid* of that. His heart. You always have been. What he wants *in his heart*.

> **EMPTY**
>
> I'm not. I know what he . . .

It's hard to say what he wants, because he's trained himself not to have an, an image in his head about what that is, what that'll be when it arrives. He doesn't need to know what he *wants*, he needs to know what he wants *to happen*. What he cares about is *process*, not some distant dreamy far-off goal. He knows that he was born to help sweep it all away—profit and exploitation, and more than that. He wants to change *everything*: how things get done, *why* we act, who's doing the acting, who we are, how we understand ourselves, all our assumptions, the ones that lie in us, marrow-deep, that determine, I mean help shape our actions. He wants all of that to change. Nothing else matters to him, because what he *knows* is that nothing else suffices. Only complete transformation.

Revolution.

(little pause)

And, and there's a profound faith in that, you know? In his willed blindness to consequence. There's a profound belief in people in him, and I love that about him, maybe more than anything else about him, his undefeated faith in a human future. That will come only when the leap is made. With the requisite, um, ferocity and strength and, and ruthlessness—or no, he isn't— With *intelligence*. He believes the world can— the world *will* be made just, as just, as fair and as human as possible. How much is possible doesn't concern him, he won't allow that to dishearten him.

That doesn't make him a joke.

(Adam takes her hand.)

ADAM

You are brave and good.

EMPTY

A whole year. I abandoned him. My father says he wants to kill himself and I tumble downstairs for a comfort fuck.

You have to think the way he does to, to understand, and
I understand him. I've always been able to follow him.
He's killing himself because of the house, so we kill the deal.
(cont'd below:)

ADAM

It's not that easy, we can't—

EMPTY *(cont'd from above)*

And we get his brain tested. And Clio and I take turns watching him. Till the baby comes. I'm going to be there, with Maeve,
for the baby, he has no right to expect me to, to . . .

ADAM

Whatever happens. Empty, you know. I will always always take
you back.

(Little pause. She looks at him.)

EMPTY

Uh-huh.
Tell the buyer I want to talk to him.

ADAM

It's a, a consortium, it's, like there isn't one specific— *(cont'd
below:)*

EMPTY

I can talk to one of the principals.

ADAM *(cont'd from above)*

And anyway it's Friday, the weekend, their office won't—
They're grabbing up property all over Brooklyn. God knows
where the cash is coming from.

Scene Four*

Pill and Eli are in Eli's small studio apartment—a single room, really, in a SRO (single room occupancy), a sink but no bathroom—on West 48th Street between 8th and 9th Avenues in Manhattan. The room's largely taken up by Eli's bed, on which Eli is lying, slowly counting six hundred dollars' worth of twenty-dollar bills. Pill's standing by the door, watching him do this.

PILL

I haven't read any of this in a long time, since . . . not even in college. Summer camp.

ELI

You read Marx at . . . ?

*See Act One, Scene Four: Pre-Scene, page 277.

(Pill nods.)

ELI

Okay, so . . . ?
Go.

PILL

A worker puts his life into what he makes—

ELI

How?

PILL

By making it, by working. His labor, his productive life goes into making objects; his labor remains in the objects in the form of value; it becomes objectified, outside of him. His life is objectified, outside of him.

ELI

Um, okay . . .

(Eli's finished counting.)

PILL

Six hundred dollars.

(Eli holds the money out to Pill, offering him the chance to take it back.)

ELI

You're sure you wanna?

(A beat. Then:)

PILL

Since man is estranged from his own labor, estranged from himself, he expresses this, as everything human is expressed, according to Marx, in relationships, his self-alienation is expressed as alienation from other men.

ELI

Yeah, right, so, all right, so—that's interesting.

PILL

The *damage* of hustling, that you're commodifying your deepest self, your capacity for giving and receiving love, romantic love, that you're turning that, that capacity within into a thing for sale, you become remote from your own—

ELI

No, not that, it's like interesting that, that if you turn tricks you're selling the alienated self. Know what I— Not like an iPhone your labor life is trapped in, like I get that, that that's bad, like I built this building I can't afford an apartment in, right, but know what I mean? It's not the building or the iPhone, it's *you*, that's the thing they buy, you don't make this thing, you make yourself *into* a thing, so—

PILL

That's what I was—

ELI

No, you were like *judging* but—

PILL

A particularly acute instance of a general affliction that—

ELI

Yeah right that's just what I mean, "acute," "affliction," but if you don't get distracted by, you know, sentiment . . . Oh I lost it— No wait, it's, it's exactly *not* that you buy this thing that has alienated worker life *hidden* in it, not concealed but,

you know, right there! You buy the alienated worker, the alienation, right, you want to fuck the alienation or get fucked by it,
the whole process of . . . what did you call it? Commodity . . . ?

PILL

Fetishism.

ELI

Cool. Like if it's an affliction, a sickness, that process, you want
to buy the process, not a boy, but a thing like a boy, in whom, in
whom—it's transparent. The affliction.
(Smiles. He holds up the money.)
Is that what you want, Pill?

PILL

You're not a boy, you're, what are you, you must be at least
twenty—

ELI

Boy, man, guy, rent-boy, hooker, whatever. What do you want
is what I—

PILL

You.
Whatever you are.

(A beat. Then:)

ELI

What I'm *not* is damaged. That's stupid, I think, it's just an
easy cliché, I'm not—I'm not even sure I'm a hustler.

PILL

You are.

ELI

No I mean when you first found me, last year— *(cont'd below:)*

PILL

Two years ago last—

ELI *(cont'd from above)*

—what was in my ad on Craig's List? I never said "generous men," um, "massage," "I'm into older dudes," any of that code. I said, I forget now, that—

PILL

"Squeeze my tits and I'll cum on your chest." Which was pretty heartbreaking I mean breathtaking. In combination with the picture. And the line from Robert Duncan.

ELI

"I have raised myself from darkness in your rising. Wherever you are."
Thank you, Yale. The four long years not entirely in vain.
I knew if someone knew where that was from, he'd . . .
You left money when we were done, and I think— *(cont'd below:)*

PILL

I'm not stupid, I could see that— This room, if I was going to see you again, that a gratuity was—

ELI *(cont'd from above)*

And I think maybe that what's freaking you out is that maybe it turns you on, paying for sex, I think the money is a, an—

PILL

It does.

ELI

Okay that's cool and maybe it turns me on too, ever think of that? Being paid for it. Who's to say that this *(holds up the money)* is an expression of our self-estrangement instead of, maybe it's an aphrodisiac, an enhancement, role-playing. Just because it's money doesn't mean it's bad; just because something's hidden doesn't mean it's bad; some people like to be blindfolded. Sometimes you like me to slap you around. I don't really want to, but you like it so I get into it. The game. Why's that different from plays, or poems, or anything metaphoric? What's the big—

PILL

But it isn't any of those things, Eli, it's really . . . real. You're a hustler. I'm a, an old dude. A john. *(pointing to the money)* That's— You can buy an iPhone with that.

ELI

I got one already so . . .

(Eli holds out the money to Pill. Pill doesn't take it.)

PILL

This . . . It's not a game, Eli.

ELI

Yeah, *I know.*
I'm not a thing. I'm not damaged, Pill. I know I'm not.
(He takes a cigar box from under his mattress. He puts the money in it.)
I got a job interning at MTV. After you left for Minneapolis. I got invited to a party where Bob Dylan didn't show. Then I was in a program for junior translators at the UN, but—

PILL

Translation? But you don't speak any other—

ELI

It just wasn't, I couldn't swing it, and a friend had an in at
ABC, said he did anyway, but, like, I don't know, I should've
stayed at MTV, which didn't pay but.
(Little pause; then, singing softly:)
"Pensa che un popolo vinto, straziato,
Per te soltanto, per te soltanto risorger può."

(Little pause. Eli smiles at Pill.)

PILL

Someone took you to the opera.

ELI

It was awesome! That little bit especially, that her father sings
to her, it was like I—I couldn't stop, you know, it moved me,
and I like, afterwards, I borrowed his CD and . . .

*(He returns to his cigar box and takes out a CD of Aida—the
whole opera, three CDs in a jewel box, not a single-CD greatest
hits—and he hands it to Pill.)*

ELI

. . . and I found that line and I memorized it.

PILL

You *borrowed* his CD.
Sing it again?

(Eli shakes his head no.)

PILL

Why'd you memorize it?

ELI

I have a fantastic memory.

81

PILL

No, but *why*?

ELI

You obviously have a theory, so . . .

PILL

What's it mean?

ELI

You know what it means, you speak Italian, you—
Oh.
Cool.
You think. You think it was for you.

PILL

Was it?

ELI

"Consider that a people, defeated, tormented,
Through you alone . . ."

PILL

"Risorger può."

ELI

"May rise again."

(Little pause.)

PILL

Would you let *me* smack *you* around?

ELI

Do you want to?

PILL

Do you let other men smack you around?

(A beat, then Eli nods.)

PILL

Whip you?

ELI

Sure.

PILL

Tie you up?

(Eli nods. They're both upset, angry.)

PILL

Burn you?
Strangle you?
Barebacking?

ELI

This turning you on?
I don't have money Pill. I can't just borrow money from *my* sister. I have to earn my— *(cont'd below:)*

PILL

You have a sister? I thought you only had a—

ELI *(cont'd from above)*

Oh, and by the way, I cost three hundred dollars an hour. *(cont'd below:)*

PILL

You raised your rent. So what, you've turned professional, full-time, I guess, you—

ELI *(cont'd from above)*
So all that money you gave me, calculating at my hourly rate, the business I lost spending my time with you? Thirty thousand dollars doesn't *begin* to, you didn't *begin* to pay for— *(cont'd below:)*

PILL
Are you advertising on escort sites now?

ELI *(cont'd from above)*
Sleeping over, sleeping over's like a thousand bucks, it's . . .

(Eli takes his iPhone out of his pocket, sits on the edge of the bed, his back to Pill; he starts texting.)

ELI
You have to leave, I have stuff to do in the morning, you should—

(A beat. Then:)

PILL
Look at you. You can type on glass.

ELI *(still texting)*
I'm . . . remarkable.

PILL *(trying to see the phone)*
Who are you— *(texting?)*

ELI *(turning so the phone's even more blocked)*
Nobody.

PILL
Let me see.

(Eli keeps texting for a beat, then stops; he hesitates, and then hands the phone to Pill.
Pill reads, scrolls down and reads some more.)

> PILL *(quiet, his worst fears confirmed)*

Goddamnit.

(He holds the phone, screen out, to Eli.)

> PILL

"Party and Play." Is that, that's meth, right, or—

(Eli angrily wrests the phone from Pill.)

> ELI

Go, Pill. I knew it, I fucking knew I shouldn't've— *(cont'd below:)*

> PILL *(over above)*

"Up for anything"? Are you out of your mind?

> ELI *(cont'd from above)*

You're a fucking hypocrite! You make me feel terrible about myself, about what I do. *(cont'd below:)*

> PILL

Good! You're putting yourself at, at terrible risk! Jesus I had no idea you—

> ELI *(cont'd from above)*

Lecturing me about my mental hygiene, which is like I dunno ironic or something! You like, first you like totally disappear on me, and— *(cont'd below:)*

> PILL

I disappear?! You, you stopped answering my calls, my emails, for, it's been six months of, of silence and—

ELI *(cont'd from above)*

—and then you show up, expecting me to— All I did was stop answering your incessant phone calls and texts, you creepy old stalker! You ran off to fucking Milwaukee—

PILL

It's Minneapolis. You know I had to. You know I did.

ELI

Why? Because that super-tense psycho-possessive queen you're married to got some job out there? *(cont'd below:)*

PILL

You were, this was bankrupting me. It was killing Paul, and, and—

ELI *(cont'd from above)*

To keep you away from me. And you went.

PILL

He's my husband. Paul's my husband.

ELI

Oh yeah right you remember that every once in a while, usually *after* you cum, funny thing, memory, huh? Your vows. You stay married to him 'cause it makes us fucking so filthy, me or whichever whore you're patronizing in Minneapolis. But it's like so so much less awesome or uniquely evil or whatnot, it's not like every other middle-aged queer who pays me doesn't have a special someone tucked away, sexual collateral in the boner bank. And the older and uglier the more likely it is that, you know, "Don't call me at home, don't act like we've met if we run into each other on the, in a bar or at some dumb musical." But, you know, blow me.

(Little pause.)

PILL

Paul and I are trying to recover what we had, reconnect, sexually, we—

ELI

Good luck! I *met* him. He's, like, *conflicted*.

PILL

He isn't. He's actually sort of great, he just—

ELI

He threatened me! He was going to fagbash me!

PILL

He was very upset. He loves me, he didn't want me to—

ELI

Yeah then whyn't he beat *you* up?

PILL

He did. I mean we had a—

ELI

Physical?

PILL

He just slapped me. Hard, he left a, a hand-shaped bruise. In twenty-six years, he never once— He lost control, he—

ELI

That's fucked up.

PILL

Even my therapist thinks I had it coming.

87

(Eli takes the six hundred dollars out of the box.)

ELI

Okay, so if you and Paul are— What's this?

(A beat. Then:)

PILL

I do love you Eli, you must know I do.

ELI

You love him. You moved out of your cool Upper West Side like
ten-room rent-controlled— *(cont'd below:)*

PILL

University housing, and it was only four—

ELI *(cont'd from above)*

—prewar apartment and went to this place where like it was in
January something like twenty-three below in broad daylight
for a week.

PILL *(moved; quietly)*

You checked. Online, you . . .

ELI

You don't love me that way.
You're the one, Pill, playing games. That's what this is: *(the money)*
It keeps it a game for you. Keeps *us* a game, an abstraction.

(Pill starts to leave.)

PILL

I . . . should go, I . . .
(he sits on the bed)
I'm lost here.
(he starts to cry)

ELI

You're . . .

I think you're crying for your dad? I think maybe you should be in Brooklyn taking care of him?

It must be like, I mean, like . . . I can't even imagine. And he's your father, you, you came out of his dick, sort of, he injected you into the womb, into the world, so, he's—tremendous to you, tremendous.

(Eli sits on the bed next to Pill.)

ELI

I missed you, I did you know, I missed how you kiss me, I miss that you'd say, you know, how intelligent I am, how . . . unlike other hustlers I was.

PILL

You aren't a—
You missed the money.
All that money . . .

ELI

I love you Pill.
I was very, um, messed up without you, I've been—
But I don't think I want to, to . . .
Never mind.

(Finally Pill looks up at Eli.)

PILL *(quietly)*

You don't want to . . . what?

ELI

I always imagined you'd see it in someone's eyes, if they really meant it. Meant to die.

(A beat. Then:)

PILL

What would you see?

ELI

I dunno, there'd be . . . some kind of light in there.

PILL

Light?

ELI *(a small nod, then)*

From, you know, the other shore.

(Pill kisses Eli, and Eli reciprocates, cautiously at first. Then it starts to heat up. They grope and claw at one another's bodies, clothing.
Then Eli stops. He pulls away.
He stands, his back to Pill, then he turns, steps back, and says:)

ELI

So, like, marry me.

PILL

I don't . . . *What?*

ELI

It doesn't have to be forever, which, by the way, nothing is, *nothing*. You and Paul: total bed death. You're pals, you're afraid to, to *look* at it. At what you guys have wound up with that expresses your self-estrangement. What you've sold for, you know, safety. Money's not the only currency.

PILL

Oh for pity's sake, Eli, what are you talking about?

ELI

It'd be insane. Pay for me. My "radiance."
(moving slowly, steadily toward Pill)
Not to rent, to own.

(Eli caresses Pill's hair.)

ELI

What do you work for now? Therapy sessions? Work to afford
me. To keep.

*(Pill stands up with an awkward laugh and steps backward,
away from Eli.)*

PILL

You're terrifying.

ELI

I am? Or . . . ?
What's hidden beneath the surface: Us.
The coolest thing about the Marxist shit is permission, you
change just your angle of sight, and there's something new,
where before there was only old . . . sadness.
You want to be sad all your life?

PILL

What's left of it.

ELI

Is that a wish?
You want to kill yourself, Pill? Like your dad?
You aren't old and ugly, I just said that.
I think all the time. When I think I think about you. All the
time. I don't want to be sad and angry for the rest of my life,
Pill. I don't want to die.

                    PILL

I don't want you to die.

                    ELI

Then . . . ?

                    PILL

Then . . .

(Eli undresses. Pill doesn't move, watching him. Eli stops.)

                    ELI

What are you doing?

(A beat. Then:)

                    PILL

Thinking.

ACT TWO

The parlor in the brownstone, early the following morning.
Maeve, eight months pregnant, is sitting with Clio at the table.
There's a small overnight bag next to Maeve's chair. On the table
in front of Clio, open flat so the cover isn't visible to Maeve, is a
beaten-up trade paperback.
In his bedroom on the second floor, above the main room, Gus,
in pajama bottoms and a T-shirt, is lying motionless on his bed,
either awake or asleep.

MAEVE

Pill borrowed money from Empty. Thirty thousand dollars.

CLIO

I see.

MAEVE

It was for our baby, we'd saved it, fertilization, super-semen. Expensive.

CLIO

I'm sure.
Not from personal experience, but—

MAEVE

It was mostly Empty's money, some mine. I'll get work soon, maybe, possibly, hopefully, who knows, I just, in March I defended the diss.

(Clio looks at her.)

MAEVE

My dissertation.

CLIO

I heard. Congratulations.

MAEVE

Thanks! Success! Maeve Ludens, Doctor of Theology! Unemployed, not exactly a bull market out there for us apophatic theologians with, you know, pronounced kataphatic inclinations.

CLIO

I wouldn't think so, no.

MAEVE

But that's me, a cockeyed kataphatist! Drives Paul *crazy*, he—
(a sudden, severe spasm in her abdomen)
OW! OW! *SPASM! SPASMSPASM! Sonofa—*

(She stands and paces, then stops by the framed photo of Congressman Vito Marcantonio. She breathes a little, then:)

MAEVE

Is that the congressman?

CLIO

Our cousin. Vito Marcantonio.

MAEVE

Oh, right. I've heard about— A *communist* congressman!
That's . . .

CLIO

He never joined the Party.

MAEVE

He looks like a movie star.
I thought maybe she'd like it, our baby having Marcantonio
DNA, but . . . That's why I went to Vito—that, and also we
couldn't *afford* anything else. That's why I wanted to kill her
when I found out she'd handed over our nest egg to Pill! So
I insisted: Vito, Tupperware and you know the needleless
syringe. And I'll find a position, later on, I'm sort of concen-
trating on gestating now, successful obstetric performance is
an uphill slog for us elderly primigravidas—I'm forty! Paul
thinks I would've found work by now if I'd avoided the mystics.
Paul, he's Mr. Systematics, you know, God the Social Worker.
He flew in from Minneapolis, he came back to Union Theological for my defense, and he turned sort of, um, incredibly
incredibly hostile. He was like trying to torpedo me. *Not* what
you expect from your faculty adviser, right? Well, he, he intro-
duced me to his sister-in-law so I'm forever grateful. So fuck
him if he doesn't, um, approve. His first question was don't
I think Dionysius the Pseudo-Aereopagite is "irrelevant."
Can you believe that? I was thrown at first, then I like *bur-
ied* him: "*Yeah*, I changed my focus to probabilism, and *yeah*,
I'm deeply into the *Dialexia de Non-Certitudine* of Juan

Caramuel y Lobkowitz. Welcome to the Via Negativa, you vengeful motherfucker." Do you know Lobkowitz?

(Clio shakes her head no.)

MAEVE

Oh I thought maybe because of of well Teresa of Ávila maybe you were into . . . I envy you old-fashioned contemplatives!

CLIO

I wasn't a . . . *(gesture: Forget it)*

MAEVE

I thought— Empty said you were a Discalced Carmelite?

CLIO

Long time gone, I was.

MAEVE

So how'd a Discalced Carm wind up with the Shining Path?! Sorry, I'm—I get curious, or, or nosy, nosy when I'm I'm nervous, and— *(cont'd below:)*

CLIO

You seem nervous.

MAEVE *(cont'd from above)*

—and my blood sugar levels these days, I'm like attic-basement, attic-basement, it's—

CLIO

I was with Túpac Amaru, not the Shining—
Okay, briefly I was with the Shining Path.

MAEVE

Holy crap.

CLIO

I read the Little Teresa of the Andes. I followed her voice, to Peru, up into the foothills, then the mountains. I learned things there; that brought me to Sendero Luminoso, to Mao, and permanent revolution.

MAEVE

Permanent?

CLIO

To overturn the world, overturn yourself. Over and over.

MAEVE

Wow! That's— That must, um, you know, *hurt*.

CLIO *(a beat, a shrug, a smile)*

Yeah. Well.

It brought me to a newfound respect for the contemplative life.

MAEVE

I respect it, contemplating, I just can't ever manage to—
Silence fucking freaks the holy shit out me. I wrote the whole diss on Xanax, but I had to cold turkey because of the *(gestures: baby)* so I'm— *(gestures: head exploding!)* I don't know why I'm drawn to the mystical Church fathers, theophany, ecstatics, inward, inward. Maybe it's because I was a drunk! Maybe all those saucer-eyed anchorites in Byzantine mosaics remind me of the gals I used to hang out with in bars, or, or maybe it's living with your niece? Maybe that's why the mystics started to attract me after I met her, she's so tough, confident, *cruel*, even, sometimes, often, and so you feel you need a a more pliable universe to take a breather in, a little *noncertitudine* break now and then from all that *certainty*.
(starting to lose it) I'm, I'm—sorry, I love her a lot, she's, she's fantastic, so elegant and beautiful and, and—
Is she upstairs?

97

CLIO

Not unless she slept on the roof.

MAEVE

Then she's . . . Downstairs.
Adam. Okay.
Not the first time THAT's happened.
(little pause, trying to keep it together)
Sober! Three years!

CLIO

That's great, hon. Good for you.

MAEVE *(losing it)*

Oh God GodGodGodGod, what am I gonna—

(Maeve starts crying, then gasping, which escalates into a full-blown panic attack. Clio watches for a moment, unrattled, then, deciding that her help is needed:)

CLIO

Just try breathing. Just breathe. In. Out.

(Maeve tries breathing with Clio, talking as she does:)

MAEVE

Yeah— I'm— This happens— It's a— *(giving up the attempt at control, back to the panic)* Oh God Oh God Oh No Oh God it's, controlled breathing reminds me of my prenatal delivery prep group *which she only ever went to with me once and then she, then she*— OH fuck oh fuck me— *(she lunges for her bag, rooting frantically in it)* I forgot to, to pack a book, reading, reading's the only thing that that calms me, slows down the cuckoo clock, sometimes, I shoulda—
(she gives up on the search through her bag, looks up, sees Clio's book) Can I borrow your—

(Maeve grabs the book and starts to read. Immediately her breathing calms down. She reads some more; she begins to find what she's reading interesting. She turns a page, reads a little more; it's very interesting. What is this book? She looks at the cover. Then, with evident surprise, she looks at Clio.)

MAEVE

Mary Baker Eddy? You're—you're kidding. You're a Christian Scientist now?!

(Clio holds out her hands for the book. Maeve gives it to her. Clio closes it and places it in her lap.)

CLIO

I don't subscribe to systems anymore.

MAEVE

Right, but, but—

CLIO

She tries to reconcile matter and the spirit. She hopes for science, and of course she fails, like Marx, but unlike him she won't surrender the spirit. And like him, in the process of failing, she makes a case for thinking instead of doctrine. Like me, she gets that there's a connection between doctrine and death: *(from memory)* "The flesh frets itself free from one belief only to be fettered by another, until every belief of life, where Life is not, yields to eternal Life."

MAEVE *(putting her hand on the baby in
her belly)*

Oh, that's—

CLIO

Yeah.

MAEVE

Beautiful. And in this house— *(mock-confiding)* —sort of heresy?

CLIO

I'll take the book with me when I go.

MAEVE

Oh.
But you're not—
You're *leaving*?

(Clio nods.)

MAEVE

Did you tell Empty? Does she—

CLIO

Not yet.

(There's a sound in the hall as V comes in the front door. In his bedroom above, Gus stirs, immediately aware.)

MAEVE

But then who'll take care of Gus?
Don't you think you ought to— Maybe she's up, I heard—

(V comes in, tense, intent, grim. He's carrying a paint-and-plaster-spattered bucket filled with tools, including a thin small handsaw, and under his arm he's carrying a square of gypsum wallboard.)

v *(seeing Maeve, immediately tenser)*

Oh.
Hey.

MAEVE

Hi, I'm . . . *(cont'd below:)*

V

Hey, Zeeko.

MAEVE *(cont'd from above)*

Coffee-klatching with your—

CLIO *(over above, to V)*

Morning, Vin.

V *(to Maeve, while putting down his
bucket and the wallboard near the
hole in the wall)*

Wow, I haven't seen you in . . . Look at you!

MAEVE

It worked! How's Sooze? How're the kids?

*(As V answers, he inspects the ragged edges of the hole, picks
bits of plaster from the exposed cracked lath, takes a folded thin
plastic dropcloth out of the bucket, opens it, spreads it on the
floor under the hole.)*

V

She's cool, she's good. Leo's a nightmare. Alice was, like, the
Buddha baby, but Leo, he's out to destroy us. He cried for a
year, spits up all his food, flunked his, you know, basic stuff,
find-the-nipple kind of tests. I wanted to leave him on the doorstep of the parish house, St. Mary's Chicken of the Sea over on
Court Street, let the priests have him. But Sooze laughs, she
thinks he's a hoot.

MAEVE

What happened to the wall?

V *(gestures to the bust, now back on the shelf)*

I shoved Garibaldi's head through it.
(to Clio) Looks like someone else took a bite.

CLIO

Gus.

(V cracks off a piece of the plaster. He takes a large chisel from the bucket and a pair of plastic goggles. He puts on the plastic goggles, and begins to chip, firmly but carefully, at the wall around the hole, squaring it off.
Gus sits up in his bed, listening.)

MAEVE

Maybe I should go into the kitchen, if there's going to be dust.

V *(brusque)*

Yeah, would you mind?

(Maeve stands and starts toward the kitchen.
Adam enters, in sweatpants and a T-shirt. He sees Maeve. Adam grins at her; she glares at him; then Adam turns to V:)

ADAM *(nervous)*

Hey, Vin.

(V keeps working, ignoring Adam.)

ADAM

I— Listen I should've told you Gus was, that he was, um—

MAEVE

Selling the house.

ADAM *(ignoring Maeve, to V)*
Of course I'd no idea that this was part of a plan to, to—

MAEVE
Kill himself.

ADAM *(to Maeve)*
You're certainly up on the latest— *(cont'd below:)*

V *(stops chiseling)*
There's something . . .

(He takes a piece of plaster and drops it inside the wall. He takes off his goggles. He taps outside the wall, about three feet down from the hole. He tries to peer down inside the wall.)

V
What is that?

(As V rummages in his toolbox for a flashlight:)

ADAM *(cont'd from above, still to Maeve)*
Oh, you talked to Empty? I mean, of course she'd call you. *(cont'd below:)*

MAEVE
She would. No matter how good you are. Stud. Bull. *(cont'd below:)*

ADAM *(cont'd from above, to V)*
Gus asked me not to tell anyone, what could I do? Client-attorney privilege, I—

V *(peering into the wall)*
Fuck! Fuck! There's something down there . . . Weird. *(cont'd below:)*

              MAEVE *(cont'd from above, heading into*
              the kitchen)

I'll make some coffee. And just . . . inhale the caffeine . . .

            V *(cont'd from above, turning to Adam)*

Privilege, yeah, right. Only . . . You ever think, like: the guy
you found wandering in the garden just a year ago, naked as a
baby, sprinkling the hydrangea bushes with his blood, this same
could-still-be-suicidal guy suddenly wants to sell his house?
You ever think, "Hey, next time I go for a drink with his son,
I'll mention it"? Or, or no such thought crossed your mind?

*(V and Maeve look at Adam; Adam looks down, then at Clio.
She's looking down at her hands on the table. Adam crumbles.)*

          ADAM *(soft, ashamed, head down)*

No, Vin. No such thought.

          MAEVE

It's Empty's too, isn't it? The, the— Are we— Is this about
the— Are we discussing the brownstone now? Or Gus?

          CLIO

It's unclear, isn't it?

          V *(over above, to Maeve)*

It's not exactly your concern, either way. Sorry, but—

          MAEVE

Come on, V, we have a baby coming, we're really—

          V

Yeah so what? I have two! *(cont'd below:)*

          ADAM

Three, actually, you have three if you count the, the new . . .
(gesturing toward Maeve)

v *(cont'd from above, to Maeve)*
And know what? I don't need half a million to raise 'em! *(cont'd below:)*

MAEVE
No, V, you just need a four-story brownstone with a garden in—

v *(cont'd from above, to Adam)*
I don't! Count . . . (gesture in Maeve's general direction) that!

ADAM *(over above, to Maeve)*
It's his family home, Maeve, it's history, it's—

MAEVE *(gesturing to her pregnant self)*
Well isn't *this* family? *(to V)* What do you mean, *"This* doesn't count"?! My baby counts! Obviously you can't deal with, with your role in the, the process of conception.

v *(a nasty laugh)*
Process? Sure, *process* is one word for it. There are other words for it. For what we did.

(Maeve glances alarmed at Adam.)

ADAM
I can keep a secret. I think I've proved that.

(Maeve looks at Clio and then goes into the kitchen.
In his bedroom above, Gus stands up. He goes to the little table he uses as a desk, picks up his volume of Horace's Epistles, *and, carrying the book, he leaves his bedroom and walks down the stairs.)*

CLIO
I take it Empty doesn't know.

V

You're so quiet, it's easy to forget you're there. *(he slams the wall)*
Maeve came over for the, y'know, jizz donation. I got home late and she was there before I had a chance to— *(jerking-off gesture)* I found it . . . provocative, so.

ADAM

Maeve is a reckless and fundamentally destructive—

V *(tired of him, swatting him away)*

Aw shut up, Adam.
(to Clio) I didn't do it to hurt Empty, or anyway it was a big big mistake and—

(Gus enters, stops, taking in the room. V goes back to the hole, chipping angrily at the plaster.)

GUS *(to Adam)*

Where's Empty? I want to show her something. *(cont'd below:)*

ADAM

She's getting—

GUS *(cont'd from above, to V)*

You're cleaning that up. Good. It's distressing to look at.

V *(working, not looking at Gus)*

Gotta make it nice for the new owner.

ADAM *(to Gus)*

How real is this?

GUS

Real is what?

ADAM

No seriously! Think how I'd feel if we'd gone to closing and then after, you'd—

GUS

Instantly she enlists the enlistable. Don't worry about what's not your—

ADAM

Last year I used my own pajama top to you know bandage your wrists, I think it *is*—

GUS *(suddenly VERY angry)*

It's *my* house, you're *my* lawyer, we did due diligence, inspections. I got a signed contract! *(To the room, but meant for V)* It's money, that's all it ever was, this house, that's all all of it is!

(V drops his tools and heads for the front door.)

GUS *(calling after him)*

You don't want to . . . You don't want to take your, your chisel? Your *saw*?!

(V slams the door on his way out.)

GUS *(to Adam)*

You don't get to have feelings! Do your job!

(Maeve comes in from the kitchen.)

GUS

Huh. Maeve.

MAEVE

Gus.

GUS

Been months, you should come around more often.

MAEVE

Don't kill yourself and I will.

GUS

Deal! Now, however, it's kinda . . .

MAEVE

Early?

GUS

Crowded! You can't swing a dead cat around here without—

(Empty enters. Silence greets her.)

EMPTY *(to Gus)*

What are you screaming about?
(to Clio) Good, you're— I want to get a second to talk to you,
about, about . . . *(cont'd below:)*

CLIO

Good. I wanted to talk, last night, but you got busy elsewhere.

EMPTY *(cont'd from above, taking in V's
mess by the wall; to Adam)*

You were right. He . . . left?

GUS

As if the very devil.

CLIO

He says there's something lodged in there.

(Empty tries to look inside the wall.)

GUS *(to Empty)*

Don't make it bigger, leave it for V to— *(cont'd below:)*

MAEVE *(over above, to Empty)*

Pill didn't come home either. *(cont'd below:)*

EMPTY

He didn't? Oh God, that's— What did Paul—

MAEVE *(cont'd from above)*

Paul waited. I waited.

GUS *(cont'd from above, holding the Horace out to Empty)*

Here, you know what else I forgot?

EMPTY *(over above, to Maeve)*

I told you I was going to—
(to Gus) Hang on a—

MAEVE

You said you'd sleep on the couch. *(cont'd below:)*

EMPTY

I did.

GUS *(over above, to Clio, indicating Maeve)*

Who invited her?

ADAM *(over Gus above, to Empty)*

Yeah, after we—
Sorry, I should butt out.

CLIO *(over Adam above, to Gus)*

She was worried. Empty should take her back to their place.

     MAEVE *(cont'd from above, to Empty)*
Far be it from *me* to— You can fuck anyone you want.

     GUS *(over above, to Clio)*
Empty can stay one more night, she can spare that.

     EMPTY *(over above, to Maeve)*
Why'd you come here? You *never* come here.

     MAEVE *(brandishing the overnight bag)*
I came to— *(to Gus)* I invited myself. *(to Empty)* I came to
bring you fresh underwear and a bra— *(cont'd below:)*

     EMPTY
You didn't have to . . .

     MAEVE *(cont'd from above)*
—and some, some trail mix, since you're the only Italians on
the fucking planet who can't cook a fucking egg.

     GUS *(to Clio)*
You want to go, you should.

     EMPTY *(to Clio)*
Go where?

     MAEVE *(to Empty)*
You know she's leaving, right?

     EMPTY
No she—
(to Clio) You are?

     CLIO
I'm going home, kiddo.

EMPTY

But . . . *When?!*

CLIO *(a shrug)*

I don't own a watch.

EMPTY

You'll, you'll put it off, till we've worked through what we're—
When did you decide this? *(cont'd below:)*

ADAM *(over above, to Clio)*

No kidding! Heading back to Paramus? Paramus, right?

CLIO *(over above, to Empty)*

He doesn't want me here. I'm in the way now, I—

EMPTY *(cont'd from above, to Gus)*

Did you know?
(to Clio) Yes, yes, and so if you walk out on this, you're—

MAEVE *(wincing slightly, hand on her
belly)*

Whoopsadaisy . . .

(The others pay Maeve no attention.)

GUS *(to Empty)*

Drop it, drop it. I want to show you something that I—

MAEVE *(to Empty and Clio)*

Now's a perfectly horrendously inopportune moment— *(cont'd
below:)*

GUS

Oh for the love of—

111

MAEVE *(cont'd from above)*

—but maybe you could factor this in, both of you? I'm, starting yesterday I—

EMPTY *(sharply, to Maeve)*

Please! Just, you know, park it for a minute and let me— This is a, a situation, you can't come blundering in expecting me to— *(cont'd below:)*

MAEVE

I get that it's a situation! *I* wasn't the one getting laid on the sly last night! *I* was busy reading up on Braxton Hicks contractions, trying to *guess* if— *(cont'd below:)*

EMPTY *(cont'd from above, to Clio)*

I was hoping, Zeeko, I thought maybe you could . . . stick it out for—
(to Maeve) That's absolutely normal for eight months.

ADAM *(to Maeve)*

Why don't you back off a little? She's upset about—
Stop throwing your weight around!

MAEVE *(to Adam)*

WHY ARE YOU HERE? WHY ARE YOU ALWAYS— *(cont'd below:)*

ADAM *(to Maeve)*

Calm down, I didn't mean "weight" like— Or maybe I did.

MAEVE *(cont'd from above)*

DO THE PEOPLE WHO BOUGHT THIS PLACE KNOW IT'S INFESTED? ARE THEY GOING TO ROACH-BOMB YOU OUT OF YOUR NEST?

ADAM

Oh you know what, Maeve, suck my dick!

EMPTY

Get out! Adam! Do what I told you to do, NOW. You don't belong here, in this—

ADAM

I'm not the one who's— Tell it to the faithless cunt-lapping harridan you—

EMPTY You risked his life!	GUS *(turning on Adam)* Jesus, you use a mouth like that to talk shit
ADAM He lied to me!	like that to a, an expectant mother, what the fuck is wrong with—
EMPTY He waved easy money in your face is what he did! I'm ashamed of you.	*(ordering him out)* Take a hike, lowlife!
	MAEVE *(to Gus, moved,* *making sure Adam hears)* Thanks, Gus, that was . . .
ADAM Well that's typical, first we fuck our brains out, and then you're all— *(cont'd below:)*	maybe the nicest thing you've ever—
	GUS Yeah, great, how about that.

EMPTY *(to Adam)*

Never ever again! Get out before I belt you, you— *(cont'd below:)*

ADAM *(cont'd from above, to Empty)*

Okay, okay, sorry, I . . . I shouldn't've . . . I'm gonna go now . . . *(cont'd below:)*

                    EMPTY *(cont'd from above, to Clio)*
He needs his, his family— *(cont'd below:)*

                    ADAM *(cont'd from above)*
Maybe I oughta . . . look into a, a hotel . . . *(cont'd below:)*

                    EMPTY *(cont'd from above, to Clio)*
—familiar, familial surroundings— *(cont'd below:)*

                    GUS *(to Empty)*
I need no such thing, I need . . . elbow room.

                    ADAM *(cont'd from above)*
For the time, um, being . . .

(Adam moves toward the door, hoping Empty will notice. She doesn't, nor does anyone else.)

                    EMPTY *(cont'd from above, still to Clio)*
You're angry at us for leaving you alone with this and you should be, but even so, you're his sister, you can't walk out on him, and how are we supposed to manage without you here?!

                    GUS *(to Empty)*
Leave her be. She does her own thing, that's how she always was. *(the book)* Here, lemme show you this!!

                    ADAM *(over above, to Empty)*
I'm . . . I'm sorry. Empty, I'm so . . . very very sorry.

(Adam leaves.)

                    EMPTY
What, Dad?

GUS

Finally!
I couldn't sleep, I don't anymore, I'm a, a bat. So I picked up
the Epistle again, trying to finish it, the last line's very—
(to Maeve) You read Latin?

MAEVE

Early Ecclesiastical, most of my stuff's in Greek, though I'm
working on a book now, sort of— *(cont'd below:)*

GUS *(turning abruptly back to Empty)*
So here's what I forgot. *(cont'd below:)*

MAEVE *(cont'd from above)*
—takes off on my diss, about a seventeenth-century probabi-
list I wonder why I don't come over? Such a warm— *(cont'd
below:)*

GUS *(cont'd from above)*
I couldn't concentrate, all night long.

MAEVE *(cont'd from above, to Clio)*
I need to, to lie down, I've been having these, like, racking
spasms in my—is there someplace—

EMPTY *(over above, to Gus)*
You were upset.

CLIO *(over above, to Maeve)*
Empty's old room, it's got a bed. I don't use it. The room to the
left of the landing, the one with the painting of the Blessed—

GUS *(over above, to Empty)*
I wasn't! I was just . . . playing with the book, feeling the paper,
and I noticed this, this—

115

(He hands the book, open, to Empty. She takes it and looks at the pages: Latin, so she looks up.)

                    MAEVE *(over above, to Clio)*
Right, that terrifying painting of Mary, I— What do you mean, you don't use the bed?

                              CLIO
I sleep on the floor.

                              GUS
I read it, marvelous, how great. Horace.
(to Maeve, aggressive) You read Horace?

                              MAEVE
"Uerum operi longo fas est obrep—"

                     GUS *(cutting her off, to Empty)*
I started to read this, a story in . . . Fuck! Which is it?

                              EMPTY
Second Book, Second Epistle.

                    MAEVE *(over above, to no one in
                                   particular)*
As I was saying . . .

(Maeve leaves. Empty watches her go, then returns to Gus's book:)

                              EMPTY
To Julius Florus.
(to Clio, about Maeve) Where'd she go, is she—

                              GUS
Turn to the last page.

(Empty does.)

EMPTY

Okay. You made notes in the margins, and here's . . .

GUS

I translated the whole— I was reading it last night like I'd never seen it.
(pointing at V's mess) He's wrong, see, I didn't learn this because I was *bored*! I could have been a classics guy, I'd've been happy doing that, but I, but I . . .

(Gus stops, looks momentarily confused, like he's forgotten where he was going; then his silence continues as his face becomes vacant, lost. He stares at Empty, who stares back at him, alarmed, waiting. Clio does the same. The vacant look and silence go on for a scarily long moment. Then:)

EMPTY *(frightened)*

You didn't.
You stayed here to work on the docks.

GUS *(to Empty)*

Yeah.
Yeah. *(a real question)* Why?

CLIO *(also frightened, but blunt)*

Because you belonged here. You were needed.

EMPTY

This was your context.

GUS

Class. My class. Working class. Right. I . . .

*(A beat, then abruptly, he seems himself again; no sign of aware-
ness of what just happened.)*

I'd forgotten I'd already translated the whole thing. That's
dozens of hours of dictionary time. And now, ooh, like a fucking newborn! Ooh!

*(Empty and Clio exchange a quick look. Then Empty looks down
at the book. She looks up at Gus, and then starts to read.)*

EMPTY (reading)

"We hear of an upstanding citizen of Argos
whose mind was taken over by a strange idea:
he decided that his life was a play that he was watching;
sitting by himself in a theater,
laughing or moved to tears, applauding
as a wonderful company of tragedians
played out the play of his life, for him, alone."
(beat, then)
"Otherwise, this citizen was absolutely normal:
friendly with his neighbors, a good host,
a good husband, and when a servant
dropped something and broke it,
it didn't make the citizen nuts:"
(she smiles a little at the word choice)
"he was a good master, too.
In other words, this man
wasn't the kind of person
who's found drowned in a well . . ."

*(She turns the page, she reads to herself, she stops and looks
at Gus. She thrusts the book back at him, refusing to read any
more of it out loud. Gus takes it.)*

GUS *(reading)*

"In other words, this man
wasn't the kind of person
who's found drowned in a well
or who falls from a cliff.
But his family was concerned about his strange delusion,
and they cured him of it by dosing him with hellebore.
When he recovered he said to them,
'You meant to cure me but in fact, my friends, you've killed me.
That dream of mine alone kept me alive.'"
(little pause; then, to Clio)
Good, right?

CLIO

Remarkable.

EMPTY *(over above, to Gus)*

Huh.
But. The man, in the poem, the citizen. His dream kept him
alive. But you . . . don't want that. To be kept alive. You want—

GUS

It's Horace, it's two thousand years old, it's not about me.

EMPTY

It's about a man whose family is trying to kill him.

CLIO

Well . . . No. The actors on the stage are trying to kill him, he
thinks. If his life is a play, right, then his family are a bunch
of actors who—

EMPTY

That's not the point! He's, he's endangered by his family's
meddling in—

CLIO

He's in danger when the actors turn on their audience, on him, and pull him into the action. See? They—

EMPTY

They kill him.

CLIO

He *thinks* they mean to, and maybe they do. But the poem doesn't say he dies.

EMPTY

"In fact you've killed me." How can you not die if someone kills you?

GUS

You're being kind of literal, don't you—

CLIO

There's death that opens the door to new life.

EMPTY

What the fuck does that mean?

GUS *(over above)*

Right, and life that's nothing but death disguised.

EMPTY

Death doesn't open doors! That's—

CLIO

It's dialectical, it's contemplation versus agency, or, or the passive good versus action, force, it's—

CLIO

EMPTY

You can't *play around* with stuff like that in front of, of *him*, Zeeko! You've what, washed your hands of— You walk away and he does it you'll feel like you murdered him.

(A beat. When Clio responds to Empty, her absolute self-control, slightly rattled by Empty's accusation, permits some deep, scary anger almost to escape:)

CLIO

You need to settle down.

(Clio goes to her paperback, picks it up carefully; and her imperturbability is back in place.)

CLIO

I'm gonna go upstairs. Maeve's having spasms. *(again to Empty)* Did you know?
(to Gus and Empty) The way I hear it, the dialectic he's writing on, it's acting versus watching. And which one is real. Right?
(to Gus) Good job with the translation.

GUS

Thanks.

(Clio leaves.
Gus and Empty look at one another. Then:)

GUS

You shouldn't be so angry at your aunt.

EMPTY

You think maybe this isn't the right moment for *you* to lecture *me* about anger?

121

GUS

I'm not angry.

EMPTY

Oh come on! *(cont'd below:)*

GUS

I'm not! *(cont'd below:)*

EMPTY *(cont'd from above)*

Stop it already! Jesus Christ! What's going on with you?!

GUS *(cont'd from above)*

Though if you keep barking at me you could get me angry.

EMPTY

All right, all right. I just—
Last June, when you got up, out of the bathtub.

GUS

Yeah?

EMPTY

If you'd stayed in the water, ten more minutes. We wouldn't
be talking now.

GUS

Yeah.

EMPTY

Why didn't you?
Something made you stand up, get yourself out into the garden.

GUS

Yeah, I dunno, I think I hadn't thought it through. I iced my
wrists like you're supposed to, to numb the pain—*that* didn't
work—and I . . .

(he bares his scarred wrists) I lay there, bleeding, this is how I remember it, and it was— It was like I was in a dream. A dream of joy. *(cont'd below:)*

EMPTY

Oh Dad, what do you—

GUS *(cont'd from above)*

And an absolutely wild strength. Dear God how long since I felt *that*? This was like 1951, my first year in Local 1814, I lifted heavy crates all day—*we lifted them*, and it only made me stronger. I was young. Then up to East Harlem all night, to work for him. *(the picture of Vito)* Incredible thoughts went through my head, I thought, this isn't dying, not like I expected, I thought that this is how it'd feel to be, I don't know how to say it. *In the future.* There, I said it. The *force* of it, that dream. But then I had to get up, out of that tub.
It was for you that I did that.

EMPTY

Huh.

GUS

That was for you. I had to— *(cont'd below:)*

EMPTY

What do you—

GUS *(cont'd from above)*

—to try to explain. You have to understand. That could, it might help you, after.

EMPTY

Help me?
So, so explain it.

123

> GUS

You don't want to understand, you just want to stop me.

> EMPTY

Of course.

> GUS

So you'll pretend to listen. You could understand if you wanted to but—

> EMPTY

That's not comprehension, that's obedience.

> GUS

Consent.

> EMPTY

To your suicide.
You never imagined I'd . . . That I'd *agree* to you killing yourself.
You couldn't. You *know* I'd never, never—

> GUS

Yeah?
That's that then.

(Gus starts to leave.)

> EMPTY

No. No, wait! Slow the fuck down! Give me a—
I've been thinking.

(Gus stands there, then an impatient gesture: Go on!)

> EMPTY

You could have done anything, once you got the Guaranteed Annual Income, you had time to do . . . whatever you wanted to do. But instead of law school or a, a classics degree even, you organized. Night and day for them, for no pay, trying to keep union membership up, all those meetings and stupid baseball games. Even though— *(cont'd below:)*

GUS

There were successes, we—

EMPTY *(cont'd from above)*

—even though history's been against you, since the '80s, Reagan and the air traffic controllers, permanent replacement workers, right-to-work laws and containerization, globalizing, all the ground that's been lost. You kept going. But.
You were losing the Party, Dad, the whole time, or something much more important: the theory, Marx, the method. That . . . abandoned you— *(cont'd below:)*

GUS

The fuck it did! Historical materialism, you think that's—

EMPTY *(cont'd from above)*

It's led you to defeat and despair. We agree about so much, we both work with working people organizing themselves into power, into, well, into *meaning*. Making meaning of—

GUS

Yeah but we mean entirely different things by doing it, you and me.

EMPTY

And you stopped doing the work, and I haven't.
So if the method's still valid, doesn't that suggest you've made an error of belief somewhere? Shouldn't you, you know— *Lenin!* Begin, begin again at the beginning, rethink! Use the time you have, whatever time that is, get back to work, organizing, work every moment till you can't anymore, and . . .

GUS

Yeah. Good. And what?

EMPTY

Without an expectation that the working class will rise up to its historical role as agent of, you know . . .

(She doesn't want to say it. He waits; then:)

GUS

Revolution.
Give up revolution.

EMPTY

Yes. Sure.

GUS *(a nod, then)*

Why not?

EMPTY

It's a, a totem word, revolution, it's, it's a magic charm, admit it.

GUS

Why not? Maybe I can get a few Mexican dishwashers to sign union membership cards even though they don't have green cards. Or, or I can go to law school like you and, and work on the ninety-seventh failed attempt to get a meaningful national minimum wage.

EMPTY

Oh fuck you.

GUS

Or whatever's eating up all your time these days— *(cont'd below:)*

EMPTY

It's just a fancy name people give for hope, something to avoid clarity and rigor about, about how difficult change actually is— *(cont'd below:)*

GUS *(cont'd from above)*

—whatever it is made you so busy you can't cross the river or pick up a— And it's hard effort, doing what you do, and it's decent and good— *(cont'd below:)*

EMPTY

I'm— I know I should've but that's not the . . .

GUS *(cont'd from above)*

—but everything you do leaves it all *intact*, and . . . comfortable, for the people you think you're fighting but also for you. And, and yes, it's soft. You know I think that, so why not say it? It's why we haven't really talked substance in years. Everyone *profits*, even the Mexican dishwashers, they get to stay here like cockaroaches and toil for sub-minimum, and it's gruesome but it beats the fuck out of slave labor in the Juárez maquiladoras.

EMPTY

The kind of work I do, you can mock it all you want, you can call me a, a revisionist, call me Eduard fucking Bernstein. But constructing, amending, altering, I'll take my chances that it'll maybe ultimately accomplish—*The New Deal. The Wagner Act. (cont'd below:)*

GUS

Yeah, the Wagner Act! And then The Taft-Hartley Act!

EMPTY *(cont'd from above)*

The Voting Rights Act. *The Brown Decision. Roe v. Wade. (cont'd below:)*

GUS

Yeah, *Roe*, wait another year or two, another Supreme Court appointment or two—

EMPTY *(cont'd from above)*

The Air and Water Act. EFCA, which is what I— None of that's *progress*, none of that's *meaningful*? Are you really going to—

GUS

And *nothing* changes. *Nothing nothing nothing.* What you call progress, I call the prison rebuilding itself. Thickening the walls. You say I can't imagine you'd consent to me killing myself? Why wouldn't I imagine that when what you've consented to is *so much worse*?! You, you walked out on, on everything I taught you, you—

EMPTY *(snapping!)*

While you've stayed where you were when you were fifteen, stuck in a circumscribed proscribed tight little arena of formulaic cant people half as bright as you walked out on after the Twentieth Party Congress *two years before I was born*! Would it kill you to consider some other— Because this rigidity, that's what's killing—

GUS

I tried to make you my companion, my comrade, you always, from when you were a baby, practically, you understood so much. And you understood that I was too greedy for you. So you left me. And all that I knew and had taught you, all of it rejected, and when you ran out of ideas to reject and method and strategy and and . . . *communion* to reject, then even, even—

EMPTY

What? *Men?* Oh don't, don't—

GUS

I'm alone in this prison. And you're alone in yours. I knew I had
to tell Vin about the house, and. And see Pill, I guess, all the
good that ever—
Maybe it only has to mean what it means to me. Me alone.

(Gus looks at the Horace, then starts to walk out.)

EMPTY

You're driving everyone away. That's your plan.

GUS

Later. I'm— I'm busy.

*(He leaves the room and climbs the stairs. Empty follows him
into the foyer and then up the stairs behind him.)*

EMPTY

This woman, Clio told us about her, that you'd met, Michelle.
Clio said she was going to, to help you. Is that—

*(Gus goes into his room and closes his door, firmly.
Empty stands on the landing outside the door. She calls through it:)*

EMPTY

Who is she? Can I come in? Please let me in.

*(Clio comes out of the bedroom on the third floor, and starts to
descend. Empty stands in front of Gus's door as if guarding it.
Clio passes her without speaking, goes down to the first floor,
through the living room into the kitchen.
Empty turns back to the door. She puts her hand on the door-
knob but doesn't open it.
Then Maeve comes out onto the third floor landing. Empty looks
up at her.)*

MAEVE

Can you come up for just a—
Come hold me.

(Empty hesitates, looking at Gus's door.
Inside, Gus is at his desk, working on Horace.
Empty looks back at Maeve.)

EMPTY

What's wrong?

MAEVE

I'm frightened.

EMPTY *(touching Gus's door)*

I'm . . .

MAEVE

I think that when she arrives, our baby, from God or wherever she originates, she'll bring answers to every impossible
question.

(Little pause.)

EMPTY

When did you find out that it—*she*, that she's a— It's a she?

(Maeve nods yes.)

EMPTY

You insisted you didn't want to know the gender. You're so into
the . . . mystery or whatever.
I just need some time to, to—

MAEVE

Yeah, but this. *(pointing to her belly)* This is all the time there is. I got into all that stuff, vision and light, because you're so hardheaded. You gather facts. You resolve contradictions. I thought I could afford to hang out with the mysteries because I thought I had you.

(Empty starts up the stairs toward Maeve.)

Scene Two

Lower Manhattan, City Hall Park.
Eli is sitting on the cast-iron railing that encircles the park.
Pill stands on one side of Eli, Paul stands on the other. Pill and
Paul face each other.

PAUL

You're not serious.
The three of us.
You're not serious.

PILL

I am.

PAUL

I know you think you are.

PILL

You could consider it, for a moment, before launching into—

PAUL

I know this seems to you a good bright idea, a . . . revelation, even. You've pierced the cloud of unknowing, you're—

PILL

I'm not leaving him.

PAUL

Then you are leaving me.

PILL

I don't want to.

PAUL

Then you have a problem.

ELI

I told him that.

PILL

Could we . . . consider . . . experimentally . . .

PAUL *(to Pill)*

You're an infant. You're so . . . Innocence doesn't even enter into it. You're . . . *Greedy.* All all all.

(Paul stares hard at Eli.)

ELI

Hey how you doing?

PAUL

You're enjoying this.

(Eli shrugs. Paul turns back to Pill.)

PAUL *(to Pill)*

It isn't that you're stupid, God knows, it's just that with you—
(cont'd below:)

PILL

There are there are questions of heteronormativity, we talk about them theoretically but we don't *live* them. And the consequences, there are maybe even tragic consequences to not being, um brave enough to—

PAUL *(cont'd from above)*

—all the scrupling and forecasting and delayed gratification and mature surrender to the Inevitable, the preparation to greet death—with you it's all *(he flaps his hands frantically above his head)* just a, a thick cloud of flies buzzing above the head of a pig. You pig. You inhuman pig-like thing. The flies are not the pig's ideals or his aspirations, they just follow the pig wherever he goes, because, well, because he stinks.

ELI

Whoah.

(Paul stares at Eli. Then back to Pill:)

PAUL

Life with you, twenty-six years of it, am I unthinkingly adhering to you like moss on a rock? No, I'm the rock, you're the moss, and I'm used to the slow eroding action you inflict on me. *Something will erode me, why not you?* Death will come for me in some shape, so why not in your shape? Why not *as you*? Why shouldn't you be my death?

PILL

But I think this will work.

I do. It's crazy, okay, it's . . . Well it's unspeakable to ask you and I'm sorry but I, I— And you know you'll, if you work at it, he's, he's an amazing—

ELI

Don't—

PAUL *(over above, to Pill)*

You're going to make me say this in front of him, aren't you? Which is hideously cruel but okay:

I wish I could turn from you forever, I wish I was made that way, I feel preposterously weak—

PILL

Please don't . . .

PAUL

I hate myself for being secretly glad, when I was up for tenure and working around the clock, that you were busy elsewhere— *with him, I knew it*—and out of my way, I hate myself for wanting it easy. I hate my own heart that loves you. And I hate you, for making me . . . face living on without you when I'm so pathetically terrified of that. And I think you know that and I think you count on that and that's why . . . *(overwhelmed, he can't continue)*

PILL

Stop. Let's, um, let's stop and—

PAUL *(turning to Eli)*

What do *you* think?

ELI

I don't think it— *(cont'd below:)*

PAUL *(to Pill)*

He doesn't think! What are you—

ELI *(cont'd from above)*

—matters what I—

PILL *(over above, to Paul)*

He does, it's just that he's—

PAUL *(to Pill)*

He just said it, if you'd listen—

ELI *(over above, to Pill)*

I can speak for myself, you keep—

PILL

You're intimidating him.

PAUL

I'm . . . ? Awwwww! *(to Eli)* Am I *intimidating* you?

ELI

You were a lot less scary back when you threatened to beat me up. All that *talk*, it's— I kind of get now why he . . . It's kind of hot.

PAUL

Oh cool, dude, like, oh LOL, oh LMAO, oh *awesome*!, like it's like oh epic fail oh burn oh *what's the matter with you*?!

ELI

You're a theologian?

PAUL

Social theology. I study dispensationalism, I study God. Ever heard of him?

ELI

You mean like in OMFG? *That* God? You're, like, some kind of *minister*?

PAUL

I don't *believe* in God, boy, I *study* God. *(cont'd below:)*

ELI

Because you don't *sound* like a—

PAUL *(cont'd from above)*

Unlike some people I have an adult's skepticism. So, like, what about you, what do you want to do when you grow up?

ELI

If I don't actually have to believe in anything, I wanna be a theologian.

PAUL

Let me give you advice, then: If you want to be a theologian, don't marry Satan. He'll fuck up your career. I was up for tenure at UTS and Columbia. This year! But *thanks to you* we had to move and I am now a visiting nobody at the University of Minnesota Department of Gender, Women and Sexuality Studies. *(pointing at Pill)* Look at him, son. You're drowning? He's not a cork float, he's a goddamned cannonball. So how's he going to save you? He abandons things. He started his dissertation in nineteen-seventy-something—

PILL

Eight. 1978.

> PAUL

Never finished.

> ELI

He told me. I only made it out of Yale because my Comp Lit professor liked sucking me off. So I don't look down, know what I'm saying?

> PAUL

Him and me, together, raising you— *(to Pill)* I take it that's the idea?

> PILL

Do you have to, to *smother* this? Do you have to?

> PAUL

An adjunct visiting whosis and a public school teacher, our combined earning power, people raise children on a lot less, Lord knows, but *(to Pill again, very fierce)* I won't give him the gum off the sidewalk, nothing, you hear?

> PILL

Paul, I can't leave you. I never will, without you? I can't. *(cont'd below:)*

> PAUL

But haven't we finally reached that place? We sailed past all the other markers.

> PILL *(cont'd from above)*

I never really thought I was betraying you. I thought, I guess it's true, it must be true, you're so entirely at the center for me, irreplaceable, inexpungeable, indisseverable, and I trusted the money to, to, as a prophylaxis against menace, not germs but but . . .

ELI

Love.

PAUL *(taking that in; then to Pill)*

But you did betray me.

Oh isn't this an awful place?

The answer's *no*. No, Pill: *No Eli.* You and me, the all-in-all

eternally. Accept the, the diminishment, disappointment. I have.

PILL

I . . . don't . . . I can't.

(A beat. Then:)

PAUL

Uh-huh well I'm uninterested in your new, what'd you call it, oh

yeah right—a new paradigm? No. Up yours. This is it, and you

know I mean that. *Inexpungeable?* Don't bet on that. Choose.

(Paul walks to the curb and holds out his hand.)

PAUL

Taxi! TAXI!

Scene Three

A little time has passed, not much time but some. Pill is sitting on the railing staring across the street, thinking; Eli sits next to him, picking at the paint on the railing.

Pill's cell phone rings. He ignores it for several rings, then takes it out of his pocket, looks at the glowing caller-ID screen; he pushes a button on the side, silencing the phone. He puts it away and goes back to staring across the street.

Eli waits for Pill to say who the caller was, or to say something. Pill doesn't.

ELI

So . . . Should we—

PILL

See over there?

ELI

Borough Hall?

PILL

The subway stop under the, to the right, under the arches.

ELI

Yeah?

PILL

A cousin of mine dropped dead of a heart attack, on those steps, the year I was born. Congressman Vito Marcantonio.

ELI

You had a cousin who was a—
Am I . . . *(supposed to know who that is?)*

PILL

No one knows about him anymore, unless you're reasonably steeped in Left history. Which nobody . . .

ELI

Yeah, I guess. I guess I'm . . . not.
That . . . did not go well.

(Pill doesn't respond.)

ELI

What's dispensationalism?

(Pill doesn't answer.)

ELI

But I get the impression of a kind of, um, I don't know, *sturdiness*? He'll be okay, if, if—

PILL

Seven-time congressman from East Harlem. Way way Left. His first term, right on the floor of the fucking House of Representatives: "I am a radical." When he died, my father said, someone wrote in chalk on the sidewalk outside the American Labor Party on East 22nd Street: "Vito Marcantonio, you was and still are the bread of the poor people." I love that. He was like a, a—

ELI

A communion wafer. The host.

PILL *(a little surprised, impressed)*
Exactly. He was like Christ to them.

(He looks at Eli, sadly. Eli looks away, back to picking paint.)

PILL

He'd lost the previous election. The Great Depression elected him, the Cold War finished him. But he never quit. He was on those subway steps there, heading uptown from the printer's, ordering the posters for his comeback campaign. A year younger than I am now. Just . . . *(Pill hits himself in the heart, hard)*
Lots of heart disease in Paul's family. Hypertension.
After Vito dropped dead, Francis Cardinal Spellman—Franny to the chorus boys he fucked—refused him burial in consecrated ground on account of his being a communist. Vito always insisted he wasn't a party member, and my father says he wasn't, though that could just be the Party's, you know, need-to-know who's-asking paranoia, my father lies about . . . Easily.

ELI

Um, maybe we should . . . *(talk)*

PILL

But oh boy Vito voted the Communist Party line. Totally pro–New Deal, but when Hitler and Stalin signed the Nonaggression Pact he was, like, stop the buildup for this imperialist war, down with Roosevelt, down with Churchill! FDR's defense appropriations bill in 1940, it passed four hundred to one. The one opposed was my cousin Vito.

ELI

Your cousin supported Hitler?

PILL *(annoyed, impatient)*

No, of course not! The CPUSA, they were like the staunchest anti-fascists!

ELI

So then why'd Vito—

PILL

When Stalin signed the pact with Hitler—

ELI

Did your father agree, I mean did he agree with not fighting, nonaggression or—

PILL

He was, um, *five*, Eli, when they signed the—

ELI

Right, so, so he joined the Party *after* they'd, I mean he joined *knowing* they'd, like, opposed America defeating Hitler.

PILL

They *wanted* to beat Hitler, but Russia needed time to— Oh it's too complicated. Google it.

ELI

Bet you're a good history teacher.

PILL

I'm sorry that came out . . . sharper than . . .

ELI

No wonder he wants to kill himself.
I mean, that's kinda heavy.

(Pill glances at Eli, surprised as always by how quick he is.)

PILL

Uh-huh. History is.
(Little pause; he's struggling with something. Then:)
I was raised to believe you must belong, to a, a class, to a party, to
a cell or a cadre, or an identity, an affinity group, even when the
affinity becomes almost impossible to, to discern, to sustain—
you make it possible, you find a way. To belong. Because if you
have no community you mean nothing, you achieve nothing,
you *are* nothing. He believes that. My father. It's paramount.
For my sister too.
Somehow, for me, belonging to anything that deeply hasn't
been possible. Betrayal's always been my only safety, my
only . . . breathable air.

(A beat, then Eli leans into Pill.)

ELI

Belong to me. I'll belong to . . .

(Pill kisses Eli, then pulls away.)

ELI

What?

(Pill's staring down at the sidewalk.)

PILL *(very softly)*

You'll be—

ELI

What I can't hear you.

PILL

You'll—

ELI

No.

PILL

You'll be okay, you'll—

ELI

No, no, wait. I won't.

PILL

He's right, I've lost my, my, my mind.

ELI

No stop, don't look down at the—

PILL

I can't look at you.

ELI

Please Pill please. Please?

PILL

Oh God. Oh fucking hell. Oh what have I done? What? What? Why won't my . . . *(he hits his head) mind* work now, and tell me, tell me . . .

                    ELI
I don't think that you, that you realize what you've—

(Pill looks at him, scared.)

                    ELI
Nothing, never mind, nothing. Forget I . . . Nothing.

(Eli jumps down off the railing.)

                    PILL
Eli.

(He reaches out to touch Eli. Eli steps back.)

                    ELI
No, no way, no way, no . . .
(fumbling in his pockets as he's talking)
I fucked up. Oh shit I . . . I can't . . .
(he finds what he's looking for—the iPhone—and as he continues to talk, he jabs and slides with his fingers, turning it on)
I can't take any of it back now, I . . .
(he shrugs, he looks at the screen, staring, not seeing)
I fucked it up.
(He switches the phone off, staring at it, immobile, as it powers down. Then he looks back at Pill.)
I dunno, but . . . I think you'll regret this. For the rest of your life. *(cont'd below:)*

                    PILL
Oh . . . If I don't . . . *(cont'd below:)*

                    ELI *(cont'd from above)*
But oh I wish I wish you hadn't, um, said what you . . . *(cont'd below:)*

PILL *(cont'd from above)*

If I don't, Eli . . . then . . . *(cont'd below:)*

ELI *(cont'd from above)*

I wish . . . *(cont'd below:)*

PILL *(cont'd from above)*

I don't want to be alive.

ELI *(cont'd from above)*

I wish—

(finally exploding) OH PILL!!!! I wish I hadn't listened to you!

(Eli runs away.)

Scene Four

Clio is seated alone at the table in the main room, reading her book.
Gus is lying on his bed in his bedroom above.
Empty comes out of the kitchen, carrying a glass of water, and heads toward the door to the stairs.

CLIO
Shouldn't you take her to the hospital?

(Empty stops.)

EMPTY
Will you stay here with him if I do?

(Clio shakes her head no.)

EMPTY

Exactly. Someone's got to stay. So maybe you can take Maeve
to the hospital, if it comes to that. Oh, wait, you can't do that
either, I hear you've sworn off medicine now, doctors, hospi-
tals. *(cont'd below:)*

CLIO

I never said that. Do you want me to take her to the—

EMPTY *(cont'd from above)*

Back on the metaphysical crack pipe, huh? Christian Science!
Seems I dunno just fucking *silly* but I guess you're running
through the gamut of available delusions so it was inevitable
you'd—

CLIO

Fuck you, sweetheart. Go fuck yourself.

EMPTY

At last, something other than, than the Yoda routine.

CLIO

The what?

EMPTY

Yoda. *Yoda?* Skip it. Back to Paterson? The federal housing
project?

CLIO

State, not federal.

EMPTY

Federal housing too cushy for you? That's the Catholic hang-
over, right? Preferential option for the poor, the magical poor.

CLIO

I help out. That's what I do now. The small stuff. Nothing magical about any of it. I'm needed there.

EMPTY

You're needed here! But you always need to be where it's utterly unbearable.

CLIO

It's unbearable here. You'd know that if you'd been here.

(A beat. Then:)

EMPTY

Fair enough.

CLIO

For a whole year, I stayed. Now I need to go, and I'm a murderer.

EMPTY

I'm sorry, and anyway I didn't say you *were* a—I said you'd feel like a . . .
Okay I'm gonna ask you something. I've always been afraid to, but—

CLIO

Ask.

EMPTY

When you were with Shining Path?
Did you kill people?

(Clio looks at her, blank. Then she shakes her head no.)

EMPTY

Did you, did you *watch* people being killed? By your comrades?

(Clio starts to speak, then can't. Then:)

CLIO

Once.
I saw all manner of difficulty in Peru. I only ever watched, but . . .
Watching isn't not doing.

EMPTY

Right.
That Easter visit, in the late '80s, when you came from Peru,
and you screamed like a raptor at Dad in the Court Street Pas-
try Shop, like if you had a knife you'd'd've plunged it in his eye,
over some sectarian madness you were into.

CLIO

The revolutionary valor of Jiang Qing and the Gang of Four.

EMPTY

Yeah, right.
(to herself) Oh my God, what am I going to . . .

CLIO

Good question.
I left people up there, in the Andes. People in Sendero I loved,
very much, the way you love someone once you've truly met
their endurance. I ran from them. I still don't know how I man-
aged that. I went to the projects in Paterson, to protect all of
you from that demented woman. To hide from her myself.
I call it my Peruvian catechism, kiddo: Some people have to be
left on the mountain.

EMPTY

But, but not *him*.
Leave him to die if you want, if you can live with that. I can't.
I won't.

                              CLIO

Then this is an opportunity for you. To defeat death.

                             EMPTY

Better to try to defeat death than you know *(making the sign of the cross) worship* it!

                              CLIO

Yeah. I suppose.
I told a neighbor lady in Paterson my brother had cut his wrists. She gave me this. *(holding up the book) Science and Health.* The title isn't promising, but it was given out of kindness. I take kindness more seriously than I used to. I read it. I found kindness in it.
She writes a lot about death.

                             EMPTY

I bet she does. How much of that did you share with Gus?

                              CLIO

She writes that death is the idea of death.

                   EMPTY *(repulsed, alarmed)*

But, but what does that even *mean*? That death isn't *real*? Or if you believe death's real, you die? *(cont'd below:)*

                              CLIO

Either of those might be what she meant, or both.

                   EMPTY *(cont'd from above)*

Both of which options? By the way? Are complete fucking wackadoo.

                              CLIO

You don't think death needs thinking about.

                              152

EMPTY

No! The *only* good thing about death is that you don't need
to think about it. How to prevent it, yes, but not what it is.
Dead's dead. *You've given up fighting! For him! You think just
because—*

CLIO

I think he's gonna kill himself.

EMPTY *(a beat, then quietly)*

He is?

CLIO

Or maybe he won't. He'll think it over and decide.

EMPTY

You've been here a year with him, just watching him drown,
and, and worse, even, than watching, the two of you, with your
bitterness and failed deadly ideas and addled nonsense about
death opening the door to some fucking future, or to Heaven,
or— Why did I think this was safe, him being here with you?
(cont'd below:)

*(V and Sooze approach the brownstone, Sooze listening to some-
one on her cell phone, V carrying a big crowbar. He enters the
brownstone. Sooze lingers outside, talking on her cell phone in
Korean to her mom.)*

SOOZE

Neh. Arasoh. Umma, gurundeh, geegum Vinnie-gah hwanna-
geh-meechusuh.
(listens, then) Yeah, he's upset. *(listens, then)* Yeah. *(cont'd
below:)*

EMPTY *(cont'd from above)*

I love you, Zeeko, I do, but go home. Now. You should go.

(V enters the room.)

                    v

What're you two up to? Sorting out who's gonna hang with the old man, keep him from hanging himself or whatever? *(cont'd below:)*

                    SOOZE *(cont'd from above, still on the phone)*

Love to Dad. *(listens, then)* I know. Love you too. *(listens, cont'd below:)*

                    v *(cont'd from above)*

That could adversely affect the sale of the— Excuse me Zeeko.

(He shoves the table to the side. Clio barely has time to get up and out of the way.)

                    EMPTY *(to V)*

Dad's working. *(cont'd below:)*

                    v

That's nice.

(V inserts the crowbar deep inside the hole. Clio pulls her chair back to the table and sits.)

                    EMPTY *(cont'd from above)*

And Maeve's napping, V, please don't— *(cont'd below:)*

                    SOOZE *(cont'd from above)*

The kids love you back. Gunnun dah. *(listens, then)* Sarang handah. Neh.

(Sooze hangs up and heads into the brownstone.)

EMPTY *(cont'd from above, to V)*

Don't be a brat. Don't make a bigger mess.

V *(to Empty, as he puts on safety goggles)*

There's something down in there.

EMPTY

What, like a, like a, a . . . What?

V

If I knew, I wouldn't need to extricate it, would I? *(cont'd below:)*

(Sooze enters the room.)

EMPTY *(to Sooze)*

Couldn't you keep him at home? He's trying to provoke my father—

SOOZE *(to Empty)*

He's on a total tear since last night, I can't talk sense to him.

V *(cont'd from above)*

Soon we shall see, soon all shall be revealed, all lies brought to light. I hate— *(bracing his foot against the wall)* —secrets, I hate leaving a job incomplete.

(V pulls violently with all his strength on the crowbar. The wall buckles forward under the pressure, and then, with a loud tearing sound, a crack opens from ceiling to floorboard. V snorts, gives another furious, violent tug at the crowbar, twisting it as he pulls down, and a section of the wall collapses, one-hundred-year-old plaster crumbling and shattering and enveloping the room in dust. Sooze and Empty scream, then Sooze starts laughing.)

EMPTY *(to V)*

What the fuck! Are you out of your mind, look what you've—
Oh my God!

*(At the sound of the wall's collapse, Gus sits up in his bed.
Maeve calls out, hurrying down the stairs as fast as she can:)*

MAEVE

Is everyone— What happened, is everyone all right?

SOOZE

Fucking hell, V, you're crazy! Look what you did to the wall!!

*(Maeve enters the room, then ducks back into the hallway to
escape the cloud of dust. Sooze and Empty wave their hands to
fan it away. It settles on everything. On the floor beneath the
collapsed wall, a rubble-heap of plaster and broken lath. Inside
the wall, behind strands of horsehair insulation, ancient pipes,
wires, the bricks of the building's exterior wall are exposed.
V reaches in and grabs something with a handle; with an angry
growl he wrenches it loose and pulls it out.
It's a small battered leather suitcase, very old, fastened with
straps, locked with thoroughly rusted latches.
V carries the suitcase to the table and puts it down, heavily. He
sits at the table next to Clio.)*

CLIO *(to V as she stands)*

Think how disappointed in yourself you're gonna be.

*(Clio, book in hand, heads to the stairs, as Maeve returns to the
parlor, her maternity smock raised to cover her mouth and nose,
her huge pregnant belly exposed.
Clio and Gus pass each other on the stairs. Clio starts to speak
but Gus hurries past her to the first floor. She ascends to the third
floor.)*

MAEVE *(looking at the suitcase)*

What is it?

SOOZE *(over above, to V)*

Open it, at least.
(to Maeve) Put down the . . . *(maternity smock)*

MAEVE *(to Sooze)*

I'm not going to breathe in all that . . .

(Gus enters. Everyone stops. He looks at the gaping hole in the wall.)

GUS

Tsk.

(Sooze gets the giggles again, controls it.)

GUS *(to V)*

How do you think that makes me feel?
Jeez, Vinnie.

*(Gus sits at the table opposite V.
V slides the suitcase toward him.)*

GUS

What is it?

V

How should I know? It's yours. The house and everything in it.

(Gus pushes the suitcase back toward V.)

GUS

I don't care.

      SOOZE *(over above, to V)*
Open it, I'm curious.

      MAEVE *(over above, to Empty, pointing*
        at the suitcase:)
That was in the wall?

      V *(over above, to Sooze)*
It's not ours.

(Sooze bursts out laughing.)

      EMPTY *(to Sooze)*
What are you laughing at?! *(cont'd below:)*

      SOOZE
It's him, he . . . breaks shit. Inanimate shit, he's not dangerous,
unless you're sheetrock. *(she starts laughing again)*

      EMPTY *(cont'd from above, to Gus)*
Do you know what's in it?

*(Outside, Paul walks up to the stoop. He hesitates, starts up the
steps, then sits, pensive. He can hear voices from inside the brownstone but not what they're saying. He listens for Pill's voice. He
takes out his cigar and puts it in his mouth, not lighting it.
Meanwhile, inside:)*

      GUS *(over the above, surveying the*
        wreckage, to V)
You're that angry. I'm amazed.

      V
I'm angrier even than that.

EMPTY *(over above, looking at the*
demolished wall, to V)
You need a therapist, V. This is scary.

MAEVE *(to Empty)*
I'm going to go make coffee, or maybe—

EMPTY
No one wants coffee now, hon, just— *(cont'd below:)*

GUS *(over above, waving at Maeve's*
raised smock)
Could you cover up the . . . ?

MAEVE
Squeamish?

EMPTY *(cont'd from above)*
If you want coffee, just . . . have some coffee, it won't—
(pointing to the water on the table) There's your water. Sorry
I— *(cont'd below:)*

(Maeve picks up the water glass, milky with dust.)

MAEVE
I don't think I'll drink it now, sorta . . . dusty.

EMPTY *(cont'd from above, to Sooze)*
I mean Jesus God, he's really lost his—

SOOZE
If you think the way he does, it's understandable, kind of. It's a
way of, of— I mean, this family. Talk talk talk but maybe tearing down a wall means more than all the—

v *(over above, to Empty, about Maeve's*
    belly)
Tell her to stop doing that.

EMPTY

Oh right, her belly's a problem but you demolish the house
and that's—

(V slides the suitcase back at Gus.)

v

Go on and open the—

(Gus throws it on the floor.)

GUS

You think this is a time for tantrums?

v

I don't know, you tell me.

GUS

This isn't a tantrum. What I told you isn't a—

v

Says you.

GUS

You're daring me now?

SOOZE

He's not daring you, Gus. *(cont'd below:)*

GUS *(to Sooze)*

No?

v *(over above, to Sooze)*
Yes, yes I am. *(cont'd below:)*

SOOZE *(cont'd from above, still to Gus)*
It'd be helpful, to him, if you'd maybe calm down a little.

v *(cont'd from above, to Gus)*
Why not? Go ahead! Do it!

SOOZE
Oh fuck I married a lunatic. Why'd I do that?

MAEVE *(over above, to Empty)*
I'm . . . *(going into the kitchen)*

(Empty's focused on Gus and V. Maeve gives up and goes into the kitchen.
Outside, Paul watches as a cab pulls up on the street in front of the house. Pill steps out of the cab and goes to Paul.)

PILL *(to Paul)*	GUS *(to V)*
Can you pay the driver?	How terrible, you carrying on like this. How badly you'll feel about this later.
PAUL *(to Pill)*	v
You don't have money?	Oh, *later!* Ominous!
PILL	GUS
I, I lost my wallet.	You're not the only one, Vin!! You're not! I have three children! You have a brother and a— *(cont'd below:)*
PAUL	
He stole your wallet. He rolled you.	

PILL
I lost my wallet. I lost
my wallet. Please.
Pay the cab.

PAUL *(Standing up,*
walking to the cab)
Damn.

(Pill looks up at the
brownstone, considering
entering. Instead he
sits on the stoop and
watches Paul pay the
cab driver. Paul returns
and sits beside Pill
on the stoop. They
don't talk.)

V
Who I dunno what *he* did—
(cont'd below:)

GUS *(cont'd from above)*
—and her, your sister.
It's a house. So we had it
a long time, so you
fixed it up—

V *(cont'd from above)*
—but he took all kinds of
money from her—
(cont'd below:)

SOOZE *(over above, to Gus)*
With you, Gus.
(cont'd below:)

EMPTY *(over above, to V)*
That's enough, V—

V *(cont'd from above, to Gus)*
I don't know the details, because between them, there's like
(holds his hands together, almost touching) this much air, if
that. *(cont'd below:)*

SOOZE *(cont'd from above, to Gus)*
With you. That's a lot of why it matters so much to him.

V *(cont'd from above)*
But she like swiped the money from their pregnancy fund—

EMPTY

I stole nothing, you little asshole, most of that money was mine, I—

V

Funny how you don't sound like someone with a kid on the way. Maeve does. You don't. What's up with that?

GUS *(rising up)*

I don't want to hear this shit, Vito, you've said enough and you made all the points you came to make, now—

(Pill takes his cell phone from his pocket and holds it out to Paul. Paul stares at it, and then at Pill, not taking the phone.)	EMPTY *(over Gus above, to V)* What's up with— You're daring your father to kill himself and— *(cont'd below:)*
PILL Please take this. Please.	GUS He didn't.
(Paul takes the cell phone from Pill. He looks at it, holding it. They keep sitting.)	V *(to Gus)* I did
PILL We should go in, or . . .	EMPTY *(cont'd from above, to V)* —and you ask *me* what's— *(To Gus) Yes he did.*
PAUL I shouldn't have come here. I should've gone up to Maeve's, and waited	GUS But that's not what he meant.

PAUL *(continued)*
till . . . Or probably
I should've gone straight
to the airport. *(he stands)*
Wash my hands of you.

PILL
I don't want to be alone.
*(almost losing it, then,
scared)* I'd better not be.

*(Paul considers this, then
nods, pockets the cell phone,
and resumes sitting.)*

PAUL
Just please don't talk.
I won't believe anything
you tell me. I can't.

V
How do you know what
I meant? *(cont'd below:)*

SOOZE
VIC FOR CRYING OUT
LOUD! SHUT IT!

*(Maeve comes back in with
a dish towel tied around her
head, covering her nose and
mouth; she's holding an
empty tea kettle and
a scouring pad.)*

MAEVE *(to the room)*
What'd I miss?

*(Pill and Paul sit. Adam walks unsteadily up to Paul and Pill
on the stoop. Adam's crocked.)*

V *(cont'd from above, still to Gus)*
It's preposterous all of this, a repeat of last summer but worse
because, because then by the time I got here you were medi-
cated and bandaged up and strapped to a fucking stretcher
and they were hauling your ass out of here, out from the, the
pools of your own blood and the places it'd sprayed on the
walls and ceiling. *(cont'd below:)*

ADAM *(to Pill and Paul)*
Hey.

PAUL
Adam.

ADAM *(to Paul)*
You know what's really hard? Trying *not* to analyze what you've done when you're trying to repent. To suffer penance, you have to, you know, *suffer*, not, not *explain*.

PAUL
Go away, Adam. Go downstairs and put your head under a—

ADAM
I've been to the Irish bar.

(Adam stands, thinking. Pill and Paul sit in silence.)

V *(cont'd from above, to Gus)*
I was so glad to see the cops, Gus, not just EMS, but siren lights and guns—
(cont'd below:)

GUS
You have to, you have to call them when—

V *(cont'd from above)*
I was surprised to find myself wanting so bad to see you *punished* by them for what you'd done, for the way you looked. I was hoping you'd kick up a fuss and they'd have to, to wail on your stupid old head with their nightsticks.

EMPTY *(to V, shocked)*
Oh come on! Don't— You don't mean that!

V
You weren't there, you didn't see him till hours later, at the hospital!

EMPTY
Because I moved out of the goddamned neighborhood, V! Who told you to stay two blocks down Clinton Street from him?

165

ADAM *(suddenly resuming)*

And I had a taco. A *fish* taco.

GUS *(to V)*

I'm sad that you saw it, I never meant for you to. You're not made for, for violence, it's . . . It's like your mother's gentle spirit, soul, whatever, was breathed into you when she let go. All your life, I protected you, assiduously, I—

ADAM

Pill, I'm so sorry that I nearly killed your father.

V

Yeah? Protected me from violence? But look how angry I get! Explain the hole in your living room. How'd I learn that?

PILL

Don't worry about it.

GUS

I kept everything from you, all the struggle, Marx and the Party and and organizing, the defeat and the victory as well, what victory there fucking ever fucking was, I couldn't bring myself to put a word of it in your ear, you have ears like her, you—

ADAM *(suddenly taking in Pill's sad face)*
Oh my God! Did he . . . ? Gus didn't do it, did he?

PILL

Don't worry about it.
(to Paul) I'm going in.
(cont'd below:)

V

Oh so sentimental when you want to be. *(cont'd below:)*

PAUL *(over above, to Adam)*
He's . . . *(indicating "Gus is inside.")*

SOOZE *(over above, to Maeve)*
Where'd Clio go? He listens to her, sometimes. Should I—

PILL *(to Adam)*
You should sleep
or . . .

*(Pill goes up the steps
into the brownstone.
In the foyer, out of
Paul's sight, he
breaks down, crying
silently. Outside,
Adam sits on the
steps, next to Paul.)*

V *(cont'd from above,
to Gus)*
You saved all your, your
mush for me, everything you
deemed worthless, every-
thing soft and and unimpor-
tant, think I didn't know that?
(cont'd below:)

MAEVE *(over above,
to Sooze)*
She's a fascinating woman.
Did you know she's a
Christian Scientist?

V *(cont'd from above)*
You kept all the, the whole crazy family's revolutionary radical
subversive brain-warping BULLSHIT— *(cont'd below:)*

SOOZE *(over V above, to Maeve)*
No she isn't, she's like a Maoist or something.
(starts toward the stairs)
Anyway, she's upstairs, usually. *(cont'd below:)*

V *(cont'd from above)*
— far from me and I thank you for it! *(cont'd below:)*

SOOZE *(cont'd from above)*
When she isn't downstairs.

*(Sooze goes out of the parlor, nearly colliding with Pill, who's
entering the main room. Sooze goes to the foot of the stairs as
Pill looks around, astounded at the wreckage.)*

V *(cont'd from above)*
I've gotten as far as respectably possible away from it without
becoming some numbskull Republican. *(cont'd below:)*

EMPTY *(over above, to Pill)*
Where were you?! Why didn't you answer your—

(Pill holds up his hand to stop her. She sees his face. She goes to him.
Outside, Adam turns to Paul.)

ADAM And know what else?	SOOZE *(cont'd from* *above, calling up)* OH HEY! HEY AUNT
PAUL *(standing up,* *to Adam)* Coffee, perhaps.	CLIO?! CAN YOU MAYBE COME—
	v *(cont'd from above)*
ADAM I'll get some, I'll come up in a, in— I'm first going down there to, well, to masturbate, that usually focuses me, then . . .	I'm a *normal* man, with a *normal life, a normal* family and a job, AN ACTUAL HONEST-TO-GOD WORKING-CLASS WORKER WITH A JOB! *(cont'd below:)*

(Paul goes up the steps and into the foyer. He listens to the fight in the main room. He considers smoking a cigar. He decides not to. He stays in the foyer, wanting to leave, unable to stop listening.
In response to Sooze's call, Clio comes out of her bedroom and starts her descent from the third floor.)

v *(cont'd from above)*
Not a, not a longshoreman who can tell me what's on page 697 of volume six of *Das Kapital* and is still, *still* in 2007 a member of the American Communist Party—

GUS

You're goddamn right I am! You never read the history of labor, you never read Marx— *(cont'd below:)*

V

You just you just *said* you kept me from it! And you did! *(cont'd below:)*

EMPTY *(to V)*

Don't mock, you could try to see it the way he sees it— *(cont'd below:)*

GUS *(cont'd from above, still to V)*

You might as well *be* a Republican. What? Because you voted for John Kerry you think you're *not?*

ADAM *(alone on the street, to no one)*

Don't tell your sister, don't tell Empty. Oh oh oh how I love her.

(Adam staggers, then descends with drunken dejection into the garden apartment.
Clio moves past Paul in the foyer and enters the living room.)

V *(cont'd from above)*

I didn't know you were a a Party member till after you quit!

EMPTY *(cont'd from above, to Gus)*

Yeah! I think I'm not a Republican because I voted for John Kerry! Who'd you vote for?

GUS

I vote for the Communist Party candidate!

V *(to Empty)*

You had to *ask?*

                    EMPTY *(over above, to Gus)*
Oh wait, oh wait, didn't the— They did! The CPUSA endorsed
JOHN KERRY! You voted for John Kerry! (to Clio) Did you
even vote?

                    CLIO
No, I never—

                    EMPTY
Skip it.

                    V
I'm amazed you had the time to vote, Gus, with your busy
schedule— *(cont'd below:)*

                    PILL *(over above, to Empty)*
What in the name of God happened to the . . . the room?

*(Empty takes Pill's hand and leads him away, into the kitchen; as
they pass Maeve, the dishtowel still covering her nose and mouth:)*

                    MAEVE *(to Pill)*
V found a suitcase in the—

                    PILL *(to Empty)*
Why does she have that towel on her face?

(Maeve takes the towel off her face.
Paul comes in, looking around the room. Sooze follows in behind
him from the stairwell.)

                    V *(cont'd from above, to Gus)*
—translating Horatian Odes night and day which you have
time to do since you don't actually work for a living!

PAUL *(to Sooze)*

What happened to the—

SOOZE

Vic was repairing the wall, after he punched a hole in it. With the bust of whatshisname, Garibaldi. Anyway he overdid it.

GUS *(over Paul and Sooze above, to V)*

Oh oh oh this is what makes me want to, to throw the hateful thing away! I raised you to make a gorgeous thing of you and a brave thing who didn't know fear and instead I, I— In my despair, in the pain! *(strikes his heart!)* In! *(strikes his heart!)* My! *(strikes his heart!)* Heart! which you dare to make mock of! And I mistakenly conceive that a gesture of my terrible, I cannot . . . describe how terrible regret at leaving you kids with the awfulness of what I'm about to do— But of course *you* can't comprehend it, I thought I was protecting you, sparing you, but all I did was make you an ignoramus!

V

Me, ignorant? *(cont'd below:)*

GUS

Ignorant, ignorant— *(cont'd below:)*

V *(cont'd from above)*

That from you, that's—

GUS *(cont'd from above)*

I should have told you all of it, like my father did to me, like, like the Depression did to me, like prison and discipline and—

MAEVE

Prison? You were in prison?

(Gus waves her away.)

                    v *(over Maeve above, to Gus)*
Right, right, so like you I could kill myself in a bathtub—
(cont'd below:)

                    SOOZE *(over above, to Maeve)*
It was during the Korean War, he was arrested for draft eva-
sion, they never talk about—

                    CLIO *(over above, to V)*
He didn't die in the tub, Vito.

                    GUS *(to Sooze)*
QUIET!

                    MAEVE *(heading into the kitchen, calling
                         ahead to Empty)*
You never told me Gus was in prison! When was that?!

                    v *(cont'd from above)*
—clutching my CPUSA card in one hand and my pension from
my Guaranteed Annual Featherbedding Fund in the—

                    GUS
And when I die it ain't gonna be in the tub! And when I do it,
don't flatter yourself, Vin, that it was because you decided to
lie down and squall like an infant over your for godsake inheritance! And you can take your "featherbedding" and shove it
up your ass, boy, you have no idea the struggle to win that, the
organizing and the strike, something else you know nothing
about—

(Empty comes back from the kitchen.)

GUS

Ask her, ask your sister, she came to the meetings, she walked with me on the pickets in the winter, she saw the scabs and heard the contempt from assholes and shitheads— *(cont'd below:)*

V

I was five years old Gus, I wanted to go with, I did, and you never took me!

GUS *(cont'd from above)*

—yelling *featherbedding* at us, because because for once we wasn't going to agree with them that they had the right to bring in fucking robot cranes and containers they built with the profits we'd made for them— *(cont'd below:)*

V

Yeah yeah yeah yeah yeah yeah . . .

GUS *(cont'd from above)*

—to replace human beings with— *Yeah! Yeah!* We did something utterly remarkable, which no one now appreciates, but it was, it was working-class guys, working-class with no, no training, no politics, facing down their own fear of being called bums and featherbedders and crooks and insisting not merely on the worker's right to a wage but the worker's right to a share in the wealth, a right to be alive, a right to control time itself! When we won the Guaranteed Income, we took hold of the logic of time and money that enriches men like them and devours men like us, and we broke its fucking back.

V

You didn't break anything! You took someone else's money that you didn't earn, that no one on Earth thinks you had any right to, and to the handful of people who know that the strike ever happened, it's a particularly grotesque example of unions abusing their power, bullies and, and mafia thugs— *(cont'd below:)*

EMPTY

That was *way* overexaggerated, just because the neighborhood was Italian-American, they— And anyway so what if the mob was involved? The issues were still—

v *(cont'd from above)*

—grabbing what they can because they can, making it impossible for American waterfronts, hell for American industry to stay profitable, to, stay *open*! *(cont'd below:)*

GUS

Ignoramus! You believe all that shit? We didn't kill the waterfront, airplanes killed that, we just refused to bear the brunt of, of . . .

v

(cont'd from above) Even when there was work for you to do you GAI guys weaseled out of it, you— You bragged about doing that, *to me*, and I acted like I knew what you were so puffed up about, I lied— *(cont'd below:)*

EMPTY *(to V)*

Okay. Stop.

v *(cont'd from above)*

—I lied to you my whole life— *(cont'd below:)*

EMPTY

V! Stop it!

v *(cont'd from above)*

—I acted like I couldn't see you'd become so habituated to shirking you didn't care what it cost you! Personally!

EMPTY *(to V)*

ENOUGH! *(cont'd below:)*

GUS *(over above, to V)*
You don't talk that way about me! I'll kick your ass, kid, I never have but don't think I won't! You're pitching shit because of the house but you may not say such ugly, ugly . . . *(he stops, exhausted or broken-hearted or both)*

EMPTY *(cont'd from above, to V)*
I dunno, *antagonism* from the workers, and you see laziness? I see anger, and if you aren't angry *for* him you need to look at yourself, nitwit, at your lifetime of easy assumption.

V *(to Empty)*
Thirty years of no vocation, *of course* there's clinical depression or senile dementia or whatever worm's boring wormholes in his brain— *(cont'd below:)*

EMPTY
It's way more complicated than that. *(cont'd below:)*

V *(cont'd from above)*
Why are you shocked? *(to Gus)* Why am I so goddamned shocked that you're a dishonorable fuck who makes promises and then snatches them away? *(cont'd below:)*

EMPTY *(cont'd from above)*
How can you be *his son* and spout that crap? Abuse of union power? What are you watching, Fox News? *(cont'd below:)*

V *(cont'd from above, to Gus)*
I oughta bill you for the thousands of hours I spent fixing— *(cont'd below:)*

(Gus starts to respond but suddenly turns away from V, from the argument. During what follows a heavy silence descends on him. He sits on a downstage dining room chair, turning it upstage so he can watch the scene continue without him.)

EMPTY *(cont'd from above, to V)*
Yeah it really is too bad about organized labor, otherwise we'd
rack up the profit margins you get from Malaysian sweatshops!
(cont'd below:)

v *(cont'd from above, back to Empty)*
Why do I wanna keep this corroding shitpile in the family?
What family? Siblings? News to me!

EMPTY *(cont'd from above)*
Unions killed American industry? You think maybe multi-
national corporations and free trade had anything to do with it?

*(Maeve comes back in from the kitchen, carrying a tray with a
filled French coffee press and mismatched mugs. She puts it on
the table.)*

SOOZE *(to Empty)*
Can I point out something? Like, just 'cause an assumption's
not easy, that doesn't mean it's *correct.* Right? Like North
Korea's run by people that share many of Gus's, um, tough
assumptions. *(cont'd below:)*

v *(over above, to Empty)*
Well no one'll ever doubt who you belong to! You drank the
Kool-Aid, and after he hangs himself with a four-million-
dollar price tag dangling from his big toe, you'll say how fucking romantic—

(Paul has noticed Gus, sitting silently; he goes to him.)

v *(to Empty, pointing to Pill)*
And whatever it is *he's* doing gets your sympathy but all I get
from you is contempt.

PAUL *(over above)*
Gus, you okay?

EMPTY *(over above, to V)*

Well listen to yourself, look at this room, whattya want, admiration? *(applauding)* Applause?

(Gus doesn't respond.
Paul looks worried.
He turns to Pill.)

PILL *(to Paul)*
I wanna get out of here.
I'll come back when—

PAUL *(coldly)*
Something's wrong with
your father. Don't you
think you ought to try to
address that. Instead of
running away? You stay
here. I'll go to Maeve's.
I'll pray you locate within
yourself the responsible,
capable adult you've
forgotten you're capable
of—

EMPTY *(to Pill)*
You really ought to stay.
Please. I know you're
very unhappy now but
please. I think he wants
you to leave. If we give
him what he wants, we're
making it possible for—

SOOZE *(cont'd from*
above, to Gus)
That's why my parents
won't talk to you anymore
Gus. They think you're
a nice guy but also they
think you're a fool.

V *(angrily snapping*
at Sooze)
He isn't a fool. Don't
say that.

SOOZE *(to V)*
Oh whoops sorry,
I like stepped in the part
of the pool reserved for you
know the Holy Family.

V
That's not what I—

SOOZE
I'm gonna go see what the
kids're— *(to Gus)* I'm
sorry Gus, you're not a fool.
I don't think you are anyway.
I just hope I raise happier
children.

(Gus doesn't respond.)

177

PILL	MAEVE *(to Paul)*
I can't.	I might go with you,
(to Paul) Please, stop.	these . . . *(gestures to her*
	belly) they're killing me.
PAUL *(to Pill)*	*(to Empty)* Maybe we all
Stop what?	ought to—

(Pill looks down, shaking his head, barely holding himself together.)

SOOZE

Aw come on Gus you know how I am, I don't blame you for Kim Jong-il.

GUS

Kind of you, hon.

PAUL *(to Empty)*

Your brother seems to want to leave again, Em, maybe— *(cont'd below:)*

EMPTY *(to Pill)*

Look at what's happening here. Can you really walk out on—

PAUL *(cont'd from above, to Empty)*

—it's finally occurred to him that the place to deal with personal business is not in public but— *(cont'd below:)*

PILL *(over above, to Empty)*

Something terrible's happened. I can't stay, I'm, I'm disintegrating.

EMPTY *(to Pill)*

Tough shit. I don't care Pill. You can't leave now, I need you to— *(she stops, turning her full attention to Paul)*

PAUL *(cont'd from above, to Empty)*

—in *private*, something else this family has perhaps insufficiently conceptualized. You're the designated driver here, Em. You really ought to consider addressing this in an appropriate fashion, take stock of the situation before . . .

EMPTY

You mean call the—

(Paul holds Pill's cell phone out to Empty.)

PAUL

911.

GUS *(to Empty)*

No more cops! (cont'd below:)

EMPTY *(to Gus)*

Okay! *(cont'd below:)*

GUS *(cont'd from above, turning on Paul)*

I'VE HAD IT UP TO HERE WITH COPS! (cont'd below:)

EMPTY *(cont'd from above, to Gus)*

Stop yelling! I get it! I don't want to call them, but how can I believe you, that you won't— Maybe, maybe you need more help than—

V *(to Empty)*

What the fuck are you waiting for? You're as crazy as he is! Call the fucking cops! *(cont'd below:)*

GUS *(cont'd from above, ignoring V, to Empty)*

You do it and I'll die hating you! I swear I will! *(to Paul)* WHO ASKED YOU? YOU INTERFERING BUSYBODY!

(Adam appears with a half-drained fifth of scotch, even drunker than before.)

PILL *(to Gus, furious)*
Don't talk to him like that!

MAEVE
Yeah Gus, Jesus, calm down. *(cont'd below:)*

v *(cont'd from above, to Empty)*
What are you— Oh of course! I didn't get it before! You don't *want* the cops here or anyone else. You want it you and him, like it always was— *(cont'd below:)*

GUS *(over above)*
Oh God another one! *(to Maeve and Paul)* BOTH OF YOU! *GET YOUR FUCKING THEOLOGY OUT OF MY HOUSE!*

EMPTY *(over above, to V)*
Oh fuck you, you malicious little spoiled petulant little—
Of course *you* don't care if he's drugged into a coma, you've always been comatose so what's the big deal? *(cont'd below:)*

MAEVE *(cont'd from above, ignoring Gus's bellowing)*
Paul's only trying to help you. My suggestion is— *(she turns from Gus to pay attention to Empty and V)*

PAUL *(over Empty and Maeve above, to Gus)*
You think God is watching this? It'll shock you and your kids but— *(cont'd below:)*

v *(cont'd from above)*

—no price too high to pay to restore yourself to your exclusive keys-to-Daddy's-Kingdom primacy over the rest of us, and, and— *(cont'd below:)*

EMPTY *(cont'd from above, to V)*

You never change! You were born whining and you never stopped! *(cont'd below:)*

v *(cont'd from above)*

—now's a good time for you to walk out on the baby that's coming and move back in here with— *(cont'd below:)*

SOOZE *(to the room)*

Isn't anyone else curious about what's in the suitcase?

PAUL *(cont'd from above)*

—watching the Marcantonios is not high on Her list of priorities. I'm over it myself. *(to Pill)* I'm going. You do whatever the fuck you want.

PILL *(to Paul)*

I don't, I don't know what to—

(Ignored by the others, Sooze picks up the suitcase. She takes it to a chair, sits with it on her lap, examines the latches, then tries to open them. They're stuck.)

EMPTY *(cont'd from above, to V)*

Who's the one who turned psycho because he broke a promise? Like he doesn't do that all the— And please, keep your snotty smutty nose out of my, my personal—

v *(to Empty)*

Maybe, maybe you could take your share of the proceeds and use it to get yourself out of your lousy— Maybe you could, you know—

EMPTY *(to V)*	MAEVE *(to V)*
I will break your fucking neck	What? What should
if you don't get a grip on—	she do with the proceeds?

(Sooze takes a bobby pin out of her hair, and tries to pick one of the locks on the latches. No good.)

v *(to Maeve)*

Was I speaking to you? I wasn't speaking to—
(to Empty) Half a million dollars, it's a lot of money. As you're aware.

MAEVE *(to Empty)*	SOOZE *(to V)*
You, you gonna respond	It's stuck. Or locked.
to that? To what he—	

(Clio, who has been watching Gus watching this, goes to him and says quietly:)

CLIO

I'm taking the Maria Addolorata painting to Paterson. *(cont'd below:)*

EMPTY *(to Clio)*	ADAM *(to Clio)*
Leave him alone.	Paterson! Not Paramus!
He doesn't care, just	
take what you—	

MAEVE *(to Empty)*

I asked you a question.

CLIO *(cont'd from above, to Gus)*
Nonna left it to me. That's okay, right?

GUS *(to Empty)*
She can take the
painting. Look what
she did for me. A whole
year.

EMPTY
Great, great. *(to Clio)*
Thanks, really, a lot, now
I think you need to—
(cont'd below:)

CLIO
I said I was going. But
first I'm gonna say good-
bye. *(cont'd below:)*

EMPTY *(cont'd from
above, to Maeve)*
I don't have to respond
to his— Can't you for
once try to put someone
else's—

CLIO *(cont'd from
above, to Gus)*
It's time, Gus. It's—
(cont'd below:)

MAEVE *(to Empty)*
Oh fuck you.
(immediately switching to V)
So, excuse me, what did
you mean when you—

V *(to Maeve)*
For the umpteen millionth
time— *(cont'd below:)*

SOOZE *(to V, brandishing
the suitcase)*
Come on Mr. Fixit, get
some WD40 and— Lookit,
something mechanical!

V *(cont'd from above,
still to Maeve)*
—it's none of your
fucking business!

MAEVE
And for the umpteen
millionth time, fuck you,
V, just—

PAUL *(to Maeve)*
I think we should both go.

MAEVE *(to Paul, waving
him away)*
In a minute.

GUS *(with a little laugh)*
Time for the fucking hellebore.

CLIO *(cont'd from above, to Gus)*
—time for me to go. I tried to go the whole march with you, comrade. I wanted to, you know that. But you're on your own path now, and it isn't mine. *(cont'd below:)*

(As Gus kisses Clio's hand, squeezing it, then letting go:)

EMPTY
Right, good, now say goodbye, say I love you and leave.

CLIO *(cont'd from above, still to Gus)*
I hope you follow it out of where you are to someplace new. Emancipation.

EMPTY
ALL RIGHT ALL RIGHT ENOUGH!

CLIO
Shouting only betrays the limits of your strength.

EMPTY
Emancipation?! Losing your last marble up on Machu Picchu doesn't give you license to, to—

MAEVE *(to Empty)*
I don't think Clio's equating dying with liberation, exactly, but— *(cont'd below:)*

EMPTY
Oh, oh, not *exactly*?! I hope my actively suicidal father's sufficiently attuned to the nonfatal nuances of her wishing him bon voyage!

(Clio kisses Gus.)

CLIO
Good night, upstanding citizen of Argos.

MAEVE *(cont'd from above, to Empty)*
—maybe if Gus could understand his desire to die as a desire for, you know, *change*, maybe then he could contemplate other means to that end, which doesn't seem to me such a terrible thing to, to— *(cont'd below:)*

PAUL *(to Maeve)*
You are *seriously* going to step into the middle of *this*? *(cont'd below:)*

(Gus pats Clio's hand.)

MAEVE *(cont'd from above, still to Empty)*
—and if you'd *tolerate*, um, for one fucking moment that people can be a little *lost* without immediately unsheathing your machete and— *(cont'd below:)*

PAUL *(cont'd from above, to Maeve)*
Did you come here expecting to be *listened to*? Have you *met* these people? There are boundaries you have to submit to, before the baby comes and she gets caught up in—

MAEVE *(cont'd from above, still to Empty)*
—hacking their heads off, maybe you could hear what she's— *(to Paul)* I'm not stepping into anything I don't belong in, *Professor Davis*, now butt out. *(back to Empty)* You, you told me he told you there'd been joy, when he, when—

EMPTY
Death's not a change!

185

MAEVE

I mean of course it *is* a change, but I but you have to see me as this bottomless sucking maw of insatiable— Fuck it! Just— *(to V)* What were you saying about the proceeds?

V *(ignoring Maeve; to Empty)*

You could buy her off with it! Just hand it over to her, so so . . .

MAEVE

So what?

V *(to Maeve)*

I'm talking to my sister! *(to Empty)* So you can run, you obviously want to! Buy your way out of the, your commitment to the baby and her.

SOOZE

Vic, that's appalling!!

PILL *(over above, to V)*
That's, that's disgusting.
(cont'd below:)

MAEVE *(over above, to V)*
Oh that is just so, so
unnecessarily vicious!
How dare you? What on
earth is the matter with—

ADAM *(over Pill and Maeve above, after
Sooze's "appalling!!" announcing
to the room)*

I just wanna say I— *(noticing the ruined wall, the room, amazement making him forget his declaration)* What happened here?

PAUL

Not now, Adam! *(cont'd below:)*

PILL *(cont'd from above, to V)*

You don't, you don't say shit like that. *(cont'd below:)*

(Sooze's cell phone rings! She pushes the suitcase off her lap, then scrambles to locate her phone.)

SOOZE

Sorry, sorry . . . *(she finds her phone, answers it, retreats to a corner)*
Hey honey. Uh-huh. Uh-huh. I know. Yeah. Mommy has to call you back. No Daddy can't talk to you now. Love you too. *(she hangs up the phone)*

PILL *(cont'd from above, still to V)*
You're out of control, shame on you.

(Clio begins to say goodbye to her nephews and niece, who are too caught up in the fight to notice.)

CLIO	PAUL *(cont'd from above, to V)*
You be good now, Pill.	And I agree! Utterly
(to V) Kiss the kids for me.	inappropriate! See,
	this is what I was saying
v *(over above, to Pill)*	about about um privacy.
Uh-huh shame on me	Oh fucking forget it.
for saying shit but where's	Might as well be talk-
your shame, for, for you	ing *to* myself.
know, whatever sick shit	
you're into that made you	
take money from her?	

MAEVE *(to Paul)*
You have no idea what shit he's capable of saying, you missed his earlier performance, he's—

(Pill starts to leave the room, then stops.)

CLIO *(to Empty)*

I was a daughter in this house too, mio tesoro. Know what
drove me out?

EMPTY *(a beat; then, deciding to ask)*

What?

CLIO

No one here knows how to forgive.

V *(to Maeve)*

And my sister doesn't wanna say anything about escaping
because, Maeve, she's so fucking angry that I'm nailing her on
it. Why do you think she's been such an astronomical bitch to
me since we, since you got pregnant with my spunk.

EMPTY *(to V and Maeve)*	ADAM
That is not remotely fair.	I think what Vinnie's trying to say is that he and—

MAEVE *(to Empty)*

It is and you know why it is. *(cont'd below:)*

(Clio walks out of the room, unnoticed.)

MAEVE *(cont'd from above, still to Empty)*

He's right, you have been a bitch to him. Because it worked.
Because it's your baby by blood. It means you can't walk out on
me when the baby arrives.

EMPTY

Which is why you insisted, I didn't want to but you *demanded*
I ask V to be the sperm donor. So that you'd be sure I'd stay.

MAEVE

Because you gave all our money, all the money we'd saved for the insemination to Pill! To sabotage our—

PILL

I'll pay back the money, Maeve. I didn't know that it was—

MAEVE

Pay us back? When?!? I'm forty years old, you think I can wait till— YOU TOOK THIRTY THOUSAND DOLLARS, THAT WAS MY BABY THAT MONEY, YOU TOOK IT AND SQUANDERED IT ON A WHORE!

EMPTY	PAUL *(to Maeve)*
No! No! You do not talk to him that way! About him that way! And in front of— Jesus Christ! The solipsism that's been blinding you since you got here— *(cont'd below:)*	And you took revenge by telling me all about what Pill was doing! What's with the high-toned indignation? *(cont'd below:)*

MAEVE *(to Empty)*

My solipsism? I've been trying to tell you that I've been feeling weird all— Up yours! *(turning from Empty to Paul, cont'd below:)*

PAUL *(cont'd from above, still to Maeve)*

And by the way I knew it all already, you just awakened the sleepwalker, for which I was grateful, if also a little repulsed by your indiscretion, no your violent—

EMPTY *(cont'd from above)*

For months now, ever since you realized you can act out with impunity because of blood sugar or the weight of its head on your bladder or—

189

     MAEVE *(cont'd from above, to Paul)*
Oh yeah right like you didn't take revenge of your own by giving me shitloads of grief about my dissertation! *(cont'd below:)*

     PAUL
Mystical light?! The hypophatic union? (cont'd below:)

*(Clio comes downstairs, carrying her bedroll, her knapsack and
a large, old, framed painting of the Maria Addolorata. She
walks past the parlor—again, no one notices her—and out the
front door of the brownstone. She closes the door behind her and
walks away down the street.)*

     MAEVE *(cont'd from above)*
Why don't you finally admit that you're *afraid* of interiority,
and the silence of God makes you panic-stricken?! *(cont'd
below:)*

     PAUL *(cont'd from above)*
You decided to get *ecstatic* after the years I spent teaching you
theology in a social context? You're goddamned right I gave
you shit about that, that hocus-pocus and—

*(Paul stops, the first in the room to notice that Gus has begun to
applaud: slow, steady, rhythmic clapping.)*

     MAEVE *(cont'd from above)*
You turned on me! And you're just jealous because while I was
willing to fight and yes *punish* for the sake of my marriage, you
were oblivious to—

     PAUL *(turning from Gus, back to Maeve)*
And I moved to Minneapolis to save my—
(to Gus) What are you doing?

(Gus keeps applauding, slowly. Everyone watches. Then:)

PILL *(to Gus)*

I'm, I'm a . . . I've been having a very rough time, and . . . I borrowed money from Empty, she gave me money and I spent it on a guy, a guy I . . .

(Gus applauds louder. Pill raises his voice and continues.)

PILL

Someone I love.

(Paul starts to walk out of the room.)

PILL

Someone whose trust I purchased, someone who I've treated, um, monstrously.

(Gus applauds louder; Pill raises his voice. Paul hesitates at the doorway, then decides to stay. He looks at Pill and Gus.)

PILL

Worse than I've treated . . . any of you, and—
(to Paul) I know, especially you, I know how badly I've—

(Paul turns away from Pill. Pill turns back to his father, who's still clapping. Pill speaks over this, past this. Gus seems to be challenging Pill.)

PILL *(with growing anger)*

You aren't nuts, or, or senile, you're fucking dissembling and— You're running away from the messes you've made, but you're not getting away without hearing me, not before I get to— *(cont'd below:)*

      ADAM *(loud, trying to get the floor)*
I think that's interesting— *(cont'd below:)*

      PILL *(cont'd from above)*
—to show you what I've done, who I am. You have to listen to
me before you—

EMPTY *(to Pill)* I don't think you should apologize for, for anything. *(turning from Pill to Gus, cont'd below:)*	ADAM *(cont'd from above, still loud)* —what Paul said about Maeve's high-toned— *(louder!)* I have some- thing to say, I—

      PILL *(to Empty)*
I'm not apologizing!

      EMPTY *(cont'd from above, to Gus)*
Dad! Dad! What are you— *(switching back to Pill, cont'd below:)*

      GUS
Applauding.

(He keeps clapping, a little less loud.)

      EMPTY *(cont'd from above, to Pill)*
Not here, not among, among people who don't wish you well—

      V *(to Empty)*
You gave him money to, to buy some hustler? Why would you
do that?

      EMPTY
None of your goddamned—

PILL

I shouldn't have asked you, Empty, and you shouldn't have said yes. He's right.

EMPTY *(to Gus, unnerved, furious, upset)*

Stop it Daddy stop doing that! You've made your point, you've made your point, it's the poem, it's the— *(cont'd below:)*

(Gus stops applauding.)

EMPTY *(cont'd from above)*

You can't bear us, you can't bear to be in the same room, in the same *world* with us, you— *(turning from Gus to Pill, cont'd below:)*

GUS

That wasn't my point, exactly.

EMPTY *(cont'd from above, to Pill)*

You're my brother! What else was I supposed to do? You begged me, you scared the crap out of me! I'm scared to be around you! *(to everyone but Gus)* You aren't *looking*, none of you! Look, look at him! If you can't get your shit together, if you can't see past your own obsessive— If you can't *see him, GET THE FUCK OUT OF HIS HOUSE*! We're helping him do it, we'll drive him to his— It's real! He's going to do it, he's going to kill—

ADAM *(VERY LOUD, to the whole room)*

V FUCKED MAEVE!
(to Empty) THAT'S WHAT I WANNA SAY! THAT'S WHAT YOU LEFT ME FOR! BETRAYED ME FOR! BROKE OUR SACRED BONDS OF—
(he notices Sooze)
Oops, sorry Sooze.

>   MAEVE *(clutching her belly, quietly)*

Ow.

>   SOOZE *(to V)*

You fucked . . . *her?*

>   V *(to Sooze)*   MAEVE

I . . . Yes.   OW.

(Sooze stares at V, then at Maeve, then bursts into a huge, pro-longed laugh.)

>   MAEVE *(grabbing her belly, not quietly
>   now)*

OW!
OWOWOWOWOWOWOWOWOWOW—

>   EMPTY

What's— What's happening, are you—

>   MAEVE

You ask me am I okay I will fucking make you eat the pla-centa! *WHAT THE FUCK DO YOU THINK IS HAPPENING?!*

>   EMPTY *(to Maeve)*   ADAM
>
> Back pain or abdominal?   Wait, I, I wasn't— There's
> Isn't that, isn't that what   more . . . I *also* wanna
> we're supposed to—   say—
> *(cont'd below:)*

>   MAEVE *(to Empty)*

You'd know what you were supposed to do, wouldn't you, if you'd come to ONE SINGLE PRENATAL— *(another sharp pain) LORD SWEET JESUS FUCK A SHIT SOUFFLE!* I'm— I'm— *(cont'd below:)*

EMPTY *(cont'd from above, looking around)*

Where's Clio? *(to Sooze)* Can you go find Clio? Is she—

SOOZE

She left.

EMPTY

What do you mean she—

SOOZE

I mean she left. Like, actually—

MAEVE *(cont'd from above)*

I'm in, I'm in— Wow, how ironic, huh? Labor *(raised fist)* and labor *(hand on belly)*. OW. Oh God, oh God, it's too early, it's too— *(cont'd below:)*

(Paul dials 911 on his cell phone. As he dials, he turns to Gus.)

PAUL

Don't panic, I'm not calling the cops.
(911 answers)
Yes, my friend, she's in, I think maybe she's in— *(cont'd below:)*

EMPTY *(to Paul)*	ADAM
Eight months, tell them it's abdominal, so maybe it's not—	I still have the floor. I just wanna say—

PAUL *(cont'd from above)*

She might be in premature labor. 537 Clinton Street, in— How long?

MAEVE *(cont'd from above)*

OW! (breathing, reciting loudly, uninflectedly, a mantra, while she holds her belly)
"Woe unto them that are with child in those days—" *(to Empty)* Yes I fucked V, it was disgusting, whaddya want from me, bitch, a fucking apolo— *(new spasm)* WHOAH! *(a little whimper, then back to the incanting)* "Ye shall hear of war and the rumors of war be ye not troubled for such things must needs be but the end shall not be yet the—" *(to Paul)* WHAT COMES NEXT?

PAUL

"These are the beginnings of sorrows."

MAEVE *(cont'd from above)*

OH RIGHT, "THESE ARE THE—" That's mis-translated, it's not "sorrows" it's "birth-pains."

PAUL *(to Maeve)*   ADAM
"Odin" is "sorrows."   I JUST . . .

(Seeing that he's not being listened to, Adam climbs up on the table.)

MAEVE

Yeah but it's "odeen" not "odin"— Because the pregnancy imagery continues: "Woe to them *that are with child and to them that give suck* in those days." *(cont'd below:)*

PAUL

Interesting.

ADAM

I JUST WANNA SAY ONE LAST THING:

MAEVE *(cont'd from above)*

"And pray that your flight be not in the winter."

ADAM *(VERY LOUD)*
I AM THE BUYER! ME! *I BOUGHT THE BROWNSTONE!*

MAEVE

You did not!

ADAM

OH YES I FUCKING DID!

MAEVE

You don't *begin* to have that kind of money!

ADAM

HA HA HA GUESS WHAT MAEVE I FUCKIN'
BORROWED IT! THE BANKS WILL LEND TO *ANYONE*!
BINGO! I BOUGHT IT!
(to Gus) ME, GUS! I OWN YOUR HOUSE! LIVE, GUS! LIVE,
BE MY *TENANT*!
(to Empty, with great passion) EMPTY!!!!! *I LOVE YOU!*

*(Empty walks up to the table, gets on it and belts Adam, hard,
in the eye. He goes down.)*

ACT THREE

Early morning, dark before dawn. Gus and Pill are in Gus's bedroom. Gus is sitting on the bed, a notebook, a pencil, the Loeb Classical Library edition of Horace's Epistles and a worn Cassell's Latin Dictionary scattered across the sheets. Pill is in a chair pulled up close to the bed, facing his father. Gus is in his underwear and a T-shirt. Pill is in yesterday's clothes.

PILL

I've always liked paying for sex.

GUS

Lots of people do that.

PILL

No, I mean . . . I like it more than, you know, sex without cash. And I don't know why my desire is married to money. To this inorganic, abstract thing.

GUS

Well, that's—

PILL

Naive, I know. Appetite and abstracted value: Angry need meets infinite possibility—that's capitalism.

GUS *(a shrug, then)*

Sort of.

PILL

Sort of. We're limited beings, human beings. Infinite possibility is something, um, many of us can't handle.
(little pause)
When I was in college I also, briefly, I took money for it. A few times. But I found I preferred consuming to being consumed.

(Little pause.)

GUS

And . . . ?

(Little pause.)

PILL

When I didn't have cash, which was often, noncommercial sex. I cheated on Paul only a few months after we'd met. I loved him and I fucked around with other guys. In the library, on the commons, our place, their places, I, I jerked off with guys on the— You want to, to hear this?

GUS

It's true?

(Pill nods.)

GUS

Lots of people do that. Cheat, I mean.

PILL

Did you?

(Gus starts to say something.)

PILL

Never mind never mind I don't want to—yes I kind of do.
Kind of.
Since . . .

(Pause.)

GUS

No. Well, once.

PILL

Wow.

GUS

Under extraordinary circumstances.
And maybe I paid for, you know, a blow job or a, a hand job
when . . . *(angry)* I don't wanna talk about it.

PILL

A blow job, you mean from like a streetwalker or—

GUS

I SAID I DON'T WANNA—

PILL

Okay! Jesus Christ.

(Little pause.)

GUS

You paid thirty grand of, of your sister's money to, just to, for sex acts? Or to spend time with him?

PILL

Yeah. To spend time. He's . . .
Today, I mean yesterday, I almost ran away with him.

GUS *(impressed)*

Madness.

PILL

Yeah.

GUS

You and Paul, he's such a sharp, straight-up, good guy. I always thought, well, you have him, you have that, a life, whether or not I approved of homosexuality, I—

PILL

Whether? Pop, you—

GUS

Still, I—

PILL

You, you told me homosexuality was symptomatic of bourgeois corruption, of *Fascism* for God's sake!

GUS

We had a different understanding, then, of—

PILL

I was *fifteen* and you told me I was like Ernst Röhm and and Goering and Goebbels, who— *(cont'd below:)*

GUS

I didn't say— I may have said that there was some sort of coin-
cidental—but— *(cont'd below:)*

PILL *(cont'd from above)*

—who by the way were *straight*! Goering and Goebbels were
straight!

GUS *(cont'd from above)*

—I never said *you* were like them! You always do that, say
I said stuff I never said.
(a beat, then:)
Ernst Röhm, though. *He* was gay.

PILL

Yes. He was. You win.

GUS

Fucking right.

*(Gus smiles; then Pill smiles back. They look at each for a
moment, then:)*

PILL

Know what's cool? The strike I've been working on, the San
Francisco dock strike in 1934? The founder of the—

GUS

You're *still* working on that? You've been—

PILL

It's my dissertation. It's late, but—

GUS

By what, thirty years?

PILL

How long did it take Marx to write *Kapital*? Fuck you.

Harry Hay, the founder of the Mattachine Society, practically the first gay political organization, he was in the '34 longshoremen's strike. And one of the strikers first killed by the cops on Bloody Thursday was a gay guy in the Maritime Cooks and Stewards Union! I found that! Okay I'm not sure he was gay but I found a picture and he looks sort of— And I've started digging into ideological splits—and I know you're gonna hate this!— between the CPUSA activists behind the 1934 San Francisco strikers and the Fourth International Trotskyists who organized the Minneapolis Truckers' Strike— *(cont'd below:)*

GUS

I *know* the Trotskyites were involved in—

PILL *(cont'd from above)*

—the same year, when there were, like, strikes all over, huge, um . . . *(cont'd below:)*

GUS

1934, yeah, almost a revolution!

PILL *(cont'd from above)*

Nationwide, revolutionary! And how those Trotskyites, free from the Comintern, they paved the way for, for socialists like Dwight Macdonald, publishing Robert Duncan, "The—" *(Eli threatens to overwhelm him, but he pushes past)* "The Homosexual in Society." *That essay*, in 1944. So like why is it that the socialists seem so much less you know puritanical, less *gruesome* about homos, about sex in general, than the Commies, why do the socialists seem so much more, um, fun? What's that dark anxiety in Leninism, that iron, icy rage that you—

GUS

Lenin abolished laws against homosexuality. Before Stalin and the—

PILL

Yeah yeah but—

I don't know, maybe—what I've been thinking is, maybe if, in some way history's just another kind of timetable, just, you know, another clock we have to punch, or, or break. Maybe the socialists felt free of that pressure in Marx and Lenin to, to force the revolutionary moment, to disrupt history? Maybe they felt free to, to imagine other forms revolution might take? *(cont'd below:)*

GUS

Huh. Maybe, but I don't—

PILL *(cont'd from above)*

I don't, it's just something I— I mean, like, for years I've wanted to ask you: in 1973, when you guys won the Income, you must've felt . . . Free of the clock, right, for the first time in your lives? That must've felt so different, like you'd become . . . I don't even know what to call it.

GUS

Workers who don't have to work.

PILL *(taking that in, then)*

Workers who don't work. That's *weird*. It must've felt amazing. *New*.

GUS

Yeah. It was. We had . . . so much *time* on our hands.

PILL

Right.

GUS

To talk over stuff, to think about stuff. For a remarkable moment.
Then . . .

PILL

In Minneapolis. Away from the guy I— Away from Eli. All
that compulsive, driven— I started working on the dissertation again. I have so much time there. It's what you fought for.

GUS

It is?

PILL

Uncontrolled, unsold, elective time . . . enters in, and moves
the angry need aside.

GUS

Are you . . .
You're not sick?
Physically, physically sick?

(Pill shakes his head no.)

GUS

What about your prostitute?

(Little pause.)

PILL

Not so far as I know. Not so far.
But that's luck, really, if he's still okay, he—
He isn't the kind of person who ought to be alone.

(Gus nods.)

GUS

Aren't you . . . Weren't you scared?

PILL

Scared of . . . ?

GUS

AIDS. Hurting Paul. Losing him. Being alone. Disappointing yourself, hating yourself. Guys who, who murder gay men. Mortification. Bankruptcy.

PILL

No, I guess I should've been but—
I'm only afraid that I gave up Eli because, deep down, I believe I'm a weak man. And I'm afraid now I'll have to prove that I was right to give him up by becoming weak. I'm afraid of becoming a fearful man.

(Gus looks at him.)

GUS

How funny, of my children, you'd be the wild, fearless one. The one unafraid. Of breaking things. I never saw before how much like me you are.

PILL *(shocked, then very moved)*

Am I?
Yeah, I guess I . . . I've never known how to live without breaking.

(Gus nods. Then:)

207

PILL

I don't understand what's really going on with you, but—
I've seen guys, back in the '80s I had friends, sick friends who
decided they couldn't bear to live anymore. I think I understand that, refusing suffering. And . . . I understand despera-
tion. "Now more than ever seems it rich to die. To cease upon
the midnight with no pain."
But . . .
I have to get out of the city, now, away from him. I don't want
you to destroy yourself, but.
I'm leaving you, Pop. To whatever you decide to do. So I don't
get a say in what you do. Because I can't stay here for you.
But don't. Please don't die.

GUS

Go home now, PierLuigi. Go home with Paul.

(*Gus turns from Pill. He puts the notebook on his knees,
opens the dictionary next to him on the bed, takes the small
Loeb edition of Horace in his left hand and with his right he
takes up his pencil. He begins to translate. Pill watches this,
then leaves the bathroom, closing the door behind him.
Pill stands on the landing outside the door, not able to move.
Empty comes up from the basement, carrying a small box con-
taining Adam's books, cups, plates. She goes through the parlor,
still last night's demolition site—debris, dust, V's tools strewn
about—and into the kitchen. The sound of the back door opening; then the sound of Adam's belongings being tossed into
the backyard. The door closes. Empty, empty-handed, comes
through the parlor, heading back down to the basement. At the
stairs, she sees Pill.*)

EMPTY

I'm packing Adam's crap.

208

(She goes down to the basement. Pill starts to follow her, then stops and returns to the landing outside Gus's door. He says through the door:)

PILL

You will be a tree. In the suicides' forest. On the second level of the seventh circle of Hell. And for all of Eternity, harpies will tear your flesh. You think about that.

(In his bedroom, Gus smiles. Pill goes down the stairs to the basement.
Sooze arrives in front of the brownstone, a red-jacketed hardcover book under her arm: Legacy of Ashes: The History of the CIA. *V follows behind her, carrying a full-size panel of sheetrock. He rests it as Sooze opens the door to the brownstone; V lifts the sheetrock and carries it inside.*
In his bedroom, Gus looks up as he hears the door opening. He finishes writing, then closes his notebook and the dictionary. He stands, the Loeb Horace in hand, a finger inserted to mark a page. Sooze looks down the stairs to the basement, listening, as V brings the sheetrock into the parlor, leaning it against the ruined wall, covering the hole. V goes into the kitchen as Sooze enters the parlor.)

SOOZE

They're in the basement, Empty and—

(She hears Gus open the bedroom door and come out onto the landing. V comes out of the kitchen with a broom and dustpan. He freezes when he hears Gus coming down the stairs.)

SOOZE

We woke him up.

V

He doesn't sleep.

(Gus enters the parlor. V starts sweeping.)

SOOZE

Sorry, Gus, sorry.

GUS

Hey hon. I thought . . .
(he goes to the sheetrock, runs his hand across its smooth sur-face, then to V) Couldn't wait till tomorrow, deliveryman?

(V ignores him, sweeping. Gus turns to Sooze.)

GUS *(holding up the Loeb)*

I finished translating. The Sixteenth Epistle.

SOOZE

Congratulations!

GUS *(opening the book)*

Here, listen to this. It's a prayer. To the Goddess of False-hood.

V *(sweeping, not looking at Gus)*

Ha!

GUS *(reading)*

"Pulchra Lauerna,
da mihi fallere, da iusto sanctoque—"

V

I don't know Latin, Gus. You didn't teach me Italian either.

210

GUS

What did you need with—

V

Pill and Empty both learned Italian.

GUS

From your mother! She taught them! Come on, V, what do you want from me?!
(the sheetrock) That's what, an apology?

SOOZE

No, but it's a—

V *(over above, to Gus)*

What in your opinion should I be apologizing for? In *my* opinion what I did was completely commensurate with the provocation, so I got no fucking—

GUS

Eh, a little less sanctimony, Vito, from a man who screws his sister's I-can't-even-say-it.

V *(flaring)*

Oh go on, say it, *I* can say it, I'm starting to think *not* saying is turning out to be not such a good—

SOOZE

V! VITO! VINNIE! VIC! *(cont'd below:)*

V *(to Sooze)*

But he's deliberately—

SOOZE *(cont'd from above)*

TRAP! *TRAAAAAAAAP!*

(to Gus) The sheetrock is a peace offering. Vin's apologizing about the wall and being a loudmouth and a douchebag. And about, you know, banging Maeve. Which I don't think was in character. I think he was kinda nutso still from you cutting your wrists, that threw him, terribly, that's maybe why he did that; I don't know *her* excuse but . . . Everybody's got one, right? He'll come by tomorrow to—

GUS

He doesn't have to—

SOOZE

He loves you Gus. You like so know he does, right? We all do. You hurt him badly. *(cont'd below:)*

V

It's okay Sooze . . .

SOOZE *(cont'd from above)*

There's something wrong with him so he doesn't know how not to make everything worse but.

GUS

Vin, I wish I could give you the house. I wish—

V

It's not the house. That's a thing, that's nothing. It's the cold-blooded lying. No, it isn't that, it's . . . because it was so easy for you to think I've been like this over a house; you think that of me. But it's not even that, not low opinion. It's rejection, the rejection that's in that. Or . . . separation, um, distance.
Not just you, Gus. All of you, all of you. My family, you . . .
(a beat, then:)
You've all always been someplace I can't go.

(V looks at the wall, the sheetrock. Gus looks at his books. He returns the Horace to the shelf. Then Gus looks at Sooze. She nods.)

SOOZE

I'll go downstairs and help pack Adam.

(She points a warning finger at V, then leaves and descends the stairs.)

GUS

I'm gonna tell you something and then you should take Sooze and go home, because I didn't sleep a wink last night and I want to.

(Little pause. V looks at Gus, suspicious.)

V

Uh huh.
Go.

GUS

The only guys who got the Guaranteed Income—

V

No, I don't care about—

GUS

Listen to me.
We had to settle with the shipping companies. We went out on strike *together*, as a union, but we couldn't beat them, so we negotiated. They gave in on the GAI, but only for employees with seniority. The younger guys . . . there were no Guarantees for them, and a year later, a lot of them, they was fired.
My friend, Shelle, um, Michelle, that you met that time?

V

Uh-huh. She seemed—

GUS

Her late husband, he died of Lou Gehrig's disease, he was one
of the younger guys who got the boot.
It was . . . for me, please believe this— *(cont'd below:)*

V

I believe you, I—

GUS *(cont'd from above)*

We won a victory for a great principle, that labor creates wealth
and should own the wealth it creates. But to win that, we sac-
rificed another principle: union. Over the years, that's come
down on me like the wrath of Heaven. When we agreed that
some, not *all* would get, we gave up the union, we gave up rep-
resenting a *class*, we became . . . Each one for himself.

V

Sometimes you have to compromise.

GUS

The best thing I ever did, Vin, was the worst thing I ever did.
And it all came out to nothing. You're right. It makes no sense
to anyone, what we did, it's written in a language no one reads
anymore, it's . . . incredible.
I see those younger men, I used to see Shelle's husband,
around? I pretend I'm old, don't see well, I pretend I don't
remember them. I pretend to forget . . . what I can't bear to
have in my head.

V

You think . . . Maybe *that's* the Alzheimer's.

GUS

I think . . . You say I'm someplace you can't go? I think that if
you don't know how to get to where I am, that's maybe the most
good I ever achieved in my life.
(little pause)
Now: Adam's gone, after your sister closed his eye, and . . .
(gesture: good riddance)
I'm not going to sell the house.

V

It's not—

GUS

I know but anyway.
I intend to keep living here.
And that's the last thing I wanna say. I'm not gonna kill myself.

(Little pause. V thinks, staring hard at Gus. Then.)

V

You're lying.

GUS

I'm not.

V

You . . . You are. You're going to do it, to try again.

GUS

No, I'm—

V

You're gonna do some awful thing to yourself.

GUS *(stern, but controlled)*
Vito, listen to what I—

V
No, no, I'm not listening to you, never again, not anymore.
I'm, I'm calling the cops. *(cont'd below:)*

GUS *(remaining calm)*
Please, Vin, don't. *(cont'd below:)*

V *(cont'd from above)*
I am, I am I don't care what drugs they put in you, I don't care
if they fucking slice up your frontal lobe if they have to—
(cont'd below:)

GUS *(cont'd from above)*
All right. I hear you. Stop now. I hear you. *(cont'd below:)*

V *(cont'd from above)*
You want me to be your jailer? I'll be your jailer, I'll do it, only
I'll hand the job over to the locked ward over at King's County
Hospital. *(cont'd below:)*

GUS *(cont'd from above)*
But Vito. I'm not. I learned things. I've seen what this is doing.
I love you kids. I'm not going to—

V *(cont'd from above)*
I will. Unless you *stop this*! I'm not going to sit back and watch
you die.
I know what you think of me, I know how . . . gullible and, that
I'm a kind of fool, I guess—

GUS
Oh baby I think no such—

V

—and I'll have to live with that but you must not, you must not lie to me about this, Gus, don't. I'm not a baby. Do you have no respect for me?

GUS

Of course I do.
I am not going to kill myself. I'm telling you the truth, heart's truth.

V

As true as that you love me?
Say that.

GUS *(a beat; then:)*
As true as that I love you, V.
(Little pause. Gus takes a deep breath, then:)
I'm asking your sister to stay tonight.
You come over tomorrow after work and we'll put up the fucking wall. Okay?

(Gus pats V on the chest and leaves the living room. He goes up the stairs to his bedroom. He sits heavily on his bed.
In the parlor, V stands alone, a long moment.
Sooze comes up from the basement, listening. Hearing nothing, she comes into the parlor.)

SOOZE

V?

(V looks at her blindly. She sees that something's very wrong. She goes to him.
Pill and Empty come up from the basement, carrying boxes. They go through the parlor heading toward the kitchen. As they pass through:)

217

PILL

Hey V.

EMPTY

Gonna tear down the rest of the house?

(They go into the kitchen. Sooze calls after them:)

SOOZE

We're going home now, he just wanted to bring over the—
(quiet, to V) What's wrong?

(V shakes his head. From the kitchen, the door opening, a crash of glass and heavy things, then another. V starts toward the door as first Empty then Pill come out of the kitchen. V stops at the parlor door. A beat, then:)

EMPTY *(to V)*

Maeve's fine.

(No response from V; he doesn't look at her.)

EMPTY

False labor.

V

Or else you'd be with her. Instead of here.

PILL

Paul's staying with her. Braxton Hicks, she was—

EMPTY *(over above, to V)*

She's fine, the baby's fine, maybe *you* should be with her, huh,
since, since—

SOOZE

He fucked her. Once. Big honking deal. Lighten up about that.
You fucked Adam the Inexplicable.

EMPTY

Okay yes I did but at least he's my ex-husband, at least Sooze
I didn't you know fuck *you*!
Jesus Christ, V!! *Your sister-in-law! What are we, hillbillies?!?!*
(cont'd below:)

v *(quietly, still not looking at Empty)*
I'm sorry. I'm sorry, okay. I—

EMPTY *(cont'd from above, to Sooze)*
I like *diapered* the motherfucker, now every time I'm in bed
with Maeve I'll have to think of, of—

SOOZE

Maybe when you're in bed with Maeve, you shouldn't think so
much.

PILL

Immemorial curse of the Marcantonios.

(Empty looks worriedly at withdrawn, silent V.)

SOOZE

What happened to the, the suitcase thing?
Doesn't anyone want to know what's inside?

PILL

Jimmy Hoffa.

SOOZE *(shrugs)*
It'll turn up, things do, they usually work out. *(gathering her
book and purse, getting ready to leave)* A couple of months

back, Alice was unhappy about Leo hogging all my time, and
Aunt Clio said to her: "Alice, there is The Cross, but also there
is The Resurrection." Which Alice, she's only three, she didn't
follow but I got it. It's not just pain, you know? Shit *happens.*

*(Sooze moves toward the door and looks at V. V stands still.
Sooze says to him, quickly, quietly:)*

SOOZE

Love you.

*(Sooze leaves the room. In the foyer she considers going up to see
Gus, then decides against it and leaves the house. Meanwhile:)*

EMPTY *(to V)*

I can't find a contract. It isn't in the basement, and even if it's
in his office, he probably already shredded it.
(Beat, waiting for V to respond, then:)
Adam. He's broken so many laws, not telling Dad that his
agent was also the buyer, for—

(V starts suddenly for the door.)

V

I'm gonna go.

EMPTY

No, wait, please, V, can't we just—

(V stops. He finally looks at Empty.)

EMPTY

He must've hidden the, that suitcase, last night? If he's both-
ered to, to squirrel it away, doesn't that suggest he's clinging to
the house, material things, his place here, on Earth?

(V shrugs, turns to the door.)

EMPTY

V, please, don't leave me alone with this.

(V looks at Pill.)

PILL

We're going back to Minneapolis. In a couple of hours.

V

Paul's going too.
Good.
(not looking at Empty) And you'll go be with Maeve?

(Little pause.)

EMPTY

He could die. Tonight. Maeve's not dying.

V

And even if she was.

EMPTY

That's . . . cruel.
I'm staying here till I know he's safe. If you can't deal with that, then, then go, I guess.

PILL *(a beat; then, to Empty)*

I know something about Gus that maybe you don't know. Though you watched how he discarded me, when I was a kid.
He loved the struggle more than me. He loves the struggle more than anything. Nothing, no one matters more.

> V *(to Empty)*

Except you.

You got everything, the roadmap to the workers' paradise, that's the real inheritance, right? Not this shitpile.

> EMPTY

He didn't lie to hurt you, probably he doesn't think he lied. There's nothing more suspect than plain simple truth, for him, he doesn't—

> V

He told me the truth.

> EMPTY *(a beat, then:)*

Okay . . .

> V

Just now. He told me why he wants to kill himself.

(V waits for Empty to respond. She stares at him. Then:)

> V

Don't you wanna know why?

> EMPTY

What did he—

> V

He betrayed half the ILU in '73, when him and the senior membership voted to take the Income for themselves. That's been eating at him for—

> EMPTY

He didn't betray anyone.

V

He *just* told me so.

EMPTY

He said no such—

V

Verbatim, horse's mouth. Considering the horse, it might be, you know, just more horse shit, but I think it was the truth.

EMPTY

He told you that he—

V

The strike, the settlement, his whole life, a waste of fucking time. He said it, Empty, to me. Now you do what you want with that. I'm through here. You think he's never kept secrets from you, but news for you: all he is is secrets, and this one, I guess the most important one of all, he told to me and not to you. Get over it.

EMPTY

He'd never say any of that, that's *you*, failing to understand, *again*, what he— He got a grubby trade union local to, to make radical demands for fundamental change, he did that, *your father*, he's a man of courage and honor, but you know nothing about that, he'll only ever be a complete stranger to you.

(V moves across the room very fast. He grabs Empty by her shoulders and slams her, hard, up against the sheetrock. He holds her there for a moment, trembling with hate. Then, as Pill runs to pull V off, Empty recovers from the shock and instantly starts punching V, kicking him. Pill tries to separate them. They tangle together as, above them, Gus, hearing the sounds of the fight, stands up from his bed. He doesn't move.)

V breaks away. Empty pushes Pill away and moves to the oppo-
site side of the room. Pill is in between.
Gus stands above them.
Pause. Then:)

          PILL *(quietly)*
Jesus Christ. Jesus Christ, V.
This is what it'll be. This is what we'll be left with, after he . . .

(They stand, not moving. No one knows what to do.
Gus stands above, listening.)

ACT FOUR

SCENE ONE

Several hours later.
Gus, Empty and Shelle are sitting at the table in the parlor.
Shelle has placed a nice, white, stiff paper shopping bag on the floor by her chair.
Gus has a small notebook. As Shelle talks, he takes careful notes.

SHELLE
Here's how you kill yourself.
These are the pills.

(She takes a medium-sized amber-colored Tupperware container from the shopping bag; it's filled with a terrifying number and variety of pills. Empty opens the container and looks inside, shaking the container a little to see the pill shapes and brands.)

SHELLE

They're the key to it. Seconal, Nembutal, Darvon, phenobar-
bytol, Xanax, Sonata, Restoril, Valium. If you have any of your
own, more than you'll need, contribute them, add to the fund.
After you . . . The idea is if you have assistance, maybe you can
make them available to someone else, if you can. *(to Empty)*
You're going to be with Gus?

(Empty doesn't look at her.)

SHELLE

These were passed to us, to my husband and me, by a visiting
nurse who got them from another ALS patient who, um, self-
delivered.
(little pause)
Which, I know, sounds like you've given birth in, you know,
out in the countryside with no one to help but . . . No.
So here are what we used, this is a box of turkey-sized baggie-
type bags.

*(She takes a box of turkey-sized baggies out of the shopping
bag. She puts one over her head.)*

SHELLE

I bought them before Thanksgiving, innocently, for the turkey.

*(She takes the baggie off her head, puts it on the table; she
returns to the shopping bag and takes out a painter's mask and
two large, thick rubber bands.)*

SHELLE

And the painter's mask. You put that on first. That's so you
don't inhale the baggie, in your nostrils or mouth, which would
make you startle and wake and start to fight.

EMPTY

Oh Jesus Christ.

SHELLE

Should I . . . ?

GUS

What else? You're doing great.
And these thick rubber bands.

SHELLE

Yeah. Those are what actually does it.
(*little pause*)
Some people take, um desiccants, um, diuretics, to reduce the
body's moisture, inhibit vapor forming in the bag—any dis-
comfort that fights the narcotizing. And the drier you are, the
less likely to vomit. Obviously don't want that! You could aspi-
rate and die from it, but . . . unpleasant.

EMPTY

And this is pleasant.

SHELLE

You'd have to ask Hal. My husband. But . . .
You sit in a chair, a recliner, or make one of pillows, so you're
not flat out, because you need gravity to work. Run the air con-
ditioner, it's faster chilly. And it's simple: Don't eat for several
hours before, pee first, take the desiccants an hour before, and
then when you're ready, you take the pills, slowly, several at a
time, with little sips of water, over as much time as you need,
but don't go too slow or you'll fall asleep before you've taken
enough.

GUS

Which is how many?

SHELLE

Eighty to a hundred.
(pause)
K, then . . . where was I? *(to Empty)* You okay?

EMPTY

Do you think he has Alzheimer's?

SHELLE

Do I . . . ? Oh, honey, I don't . . . I keep the books at Big Bear
Auto Body on Hamilton Avenue, and I do part-time checkout
at Grand Union. Do you? Think he . . . ? Didn't Gus say you're
a nurse?

GUS

Was, I said was, she's a lawyer now. Labor lawyer.

SHELLE

Oh so it runs in the family!
(Singing:)
"There once was a Union Maid, who never was afraid,
Of the goons and ginks and company finks
And the Deputy Sheriff who made the raid!"

(Little pause.)

SHELLE

My old man taught me.
I'm sorry I get silly when I'm nervous.

GUS

You're doing great. I have Alzheimer's. What's next? Eighty to
a hundred pills, and . . .

SHELLE

Then you, you sit back, sit up, don't lie down. You say whatever there is to say, or maybe do that before the pills. You put
on the painter's mask. Then the bag. Then you put the rubber
bands around the bag around your neck. And you, you . . .
Sorry.

GUS

Is that . . . ?

SHELLE

You stick your fingers. Two fingers each hand, like this *(she dem-
onstrates with her hands)* between the rubber bands and your
neck, on either side, so air gets in, so as you fall asleep, air's getting in, you don't feel suffocating, or in danger, you don't panic.
Until when you're really asleep, gravity pulls at your arms, your
hands. Your arms'll drop. Your fingers pull out. The bands close
around your neck and the air stops getting in.

(Gus looks at his hands, his fingers.)

EMPTY

So that's . . . Clever.

SHELLE

You can't touch him. Not at all. You watch. If there's police,
and there will be, they won't ask, it's suicide. But they have to
look for any sign you assisted, physically, and if you did, and
they find out, and if you did they will, they have to arrest you
and charge you with murder or manslaughter or—well you're
a lawyer so . . .

EMPTY

You watched your husband.

(As Shelle speaks she puts the ingredients back in the shopping bag.)

SHELLE

He was . . . He was in a very bad way. It's a very bad . . . Taking care of him was hard. He'd been out of work . . . Well after the strike, I told Gus this, he was a young man but he came from a family of longshoremen and getting laid off, he, he didn't have seniority so he didn't get on the Guaranteed Income, he was one of the ones got fired. And he never found a place after that. So even before the ALS, our life wasn't great, he was a burden to me, I wasn't out of high school when you guys struck, but I carried him. He had jobs, but . . . Not having an ILU union card in his wallet, it shouldn't've but it spoiled everything for him. His life. And mine.

And then *after*? He got sick? *Really* not great—his last two years.

Did I want him dead? I did. Sometimes. So when I agreed to help him, it was hard for me to be sure, um, about my lack of personal investment. In the outcome. But that's . . . I can go to Mass. I'm going now.

Whatever else, I didn't want him to be lonely. He was going where maybe he's alone. For the first time ever.

I guess I thought I ought to say that. Since I'm delivering this bag.

(Beat. Shelle stands, puts the shopping bag on the table, then goes to Gus and puts an arm around him, giving him a squeeze. He pats her hand, looking at Empty. Then Shelle sings to Gus:)

SHELLE *(singing, softly)*

"Oh you can't scare me I'm stickin' to the Union,
I'm stickin' to the Union,
I'm stickin' to the Union . . ."

SHELLE AND GUS *(singing together)*
"Oh you can't scare me I'm stickin' to the Union,
I'm stickin' to the Union,
Till the day I die."

Scene Two

Empty and Gus are alone. Shelle has just left. Her shopping bag is now on the floor by Gus's chair.

EMPTY

She seems nice.

GUS

We met in a bar. The Irish bar. She's Irish. O'Neill.

EMPTY

How come you never dated anyone? After Mom?

GUS

"You want to kill yourself because you don't have someone to go to the movies with. You want to die because you're lonely. You need some, some . . ."

EMPTY

Love. Pussy.

GUS

I hate it when you talk like a, a—

EMPTY

Longshoreman? You make me listen to . . . to her unpacking her creepy self-annihilation do-it-yourself kit and act all, I dunno, fascinated, but sex makes you squirm. You're so Victorian.

GUS

You trivialize yourself.

EMPTY

You've always been, um, heroic to me. Your willingness to endure any hardship for the good of the collective.

GUS

What good? What collective? The Union? The Party? If I go now, I can predecease it. But I better hurry.

EMPTY

Us?

(He doesn't answer.)

EMPTY

Why shouldn't I do it? If endurance is so . . . stupid, why don't we all kill ourselves now? Right now?

GUS

You don't want that baby?

EMPTY

I won't talk about that.

GUS

Funny how I never thought of you having kids. Maria Teresa.
M. T.

EMPTY

But I never did, really, I don't feel empty. Other things interest me. Always have. I always appreciated it, that you never
pathologized that, that you never seemed, um, curious, or even
interested in why Adam and I never had children. We could
contend together, you and I. We could argue, and read, I could
bring you Louis Althusser, and Chantal Mouffe— *(cont'd
below:)*

(Gus makes disapproving sounds.)

EMPTY *(cont'd from above)*

And you could give me all those, you know, solid guys, Sweezy,
and Braverman, and whatsername . . . Ellen Meiksins Wood.
E. P. Thompson.

GUS

The Making of the English Working Class.

EMPTY

I didn't have baby stories for you, I had . . . domestic worker
statistics. And so you told me your stories. We had that. And
it was so completely mine, what you told me. Stuff Mom never
knew.

GUS

No.

EMPTY

The prison stuff, I know no one else knows that.

GUS

But maybe I shouldn't've told you. Maybe I've asked too much of you, and took your life out of your hands; maybe I kept too much of you for myself.

EMPTY

Maybe.
Then how, if you think that . . . How can you contemplate *this*?

GUS *(a beat, then a shrug)*
Maybe it's so you could take yourself back. So you can get out. If you want.

(Empty looks at him, uncomprehending/not wanting to comprehend.)

GUS

Once, I'd look at the world, and where most people see only solid stone, or chaos, I could see . . . through that. The theory and the method: I could see systems, fixities; but between the fixities, I saw *forces*, of attraction and repulsion. And I could see how a balancing of these forces kept the fixed things in place, how systems survive by paralysis. Antithetical to life. And I'd learned, and I *know*, if you change the balance of these forces, if you find a way to become an agent of imbalance, instabilities will occur, fixities become unfixed. It isn't magic but it felt like magic.
(little pause)
Now I see . . . only what most people see. A system in place. I'm trapped in it, like everyone is. The injustice of the world that's triumphant now, that's been building its triumph for a long time; its triumph is chaos. And the prison is . . . I can't see an agent, a class capable of altering the balancing of forces to produce its destruction. Without the hope of that, I can't see anything of any meaning to think about and anticipate and

work towards. Either I accept that, that the future means nothing, that there is no future, and I surrender to despair, or . . .

EMPTY

Or?

GUS

I refuse despair. I apply my discipline, my training, I apply
what's left of my cold objective eye to my *(with great disgust)*
surroundings, and I free myself. *(gestures at the shopping bag)*
The only real death is to live meaninglessly, a helpless animal,
a dead thing. It isn't my death that's my despair, it's my life. My
death, my suicide, that's my hope.

EMPTY

But . . .
I have to live. I have an effect in the world, *on* the world.
I work, to, to change specific, actual conditions.
Even if you don't respect or see any value in what I do: Here
I am. I'm your child. You have to endure this life you hate. *For*
me. So that I won't be afraid.

GUS *(a nod, then)*

I make you feel safe.
Maybe for that alone I deserve to die.

(Empty's taken aback; some bell goes off. She considers what
he's said, then, uneasy, unsure, she decides against responding
directly.)

EMPTY

What you told V? About, about betraying the membership.
(cont'd below:)

GUS

No, no, that's history, it's—

EMPTY *(cont'd from above)*

I didn't believe him, that you'd told him that, that that's how you feel about— But then Shelle said that thing about her husband.

GUS

We lost and we called it a victory. I told you that it was this great thing. I knew better. I failed. I failed *you*. You fail your children when you fail the world.

EMPTY

You did the best you could for as many as you could. You have to make peace with that. I thought you had.

GUS

The hell you did. You're too smart to think that. You were afraid to ask.

EMPTY

I'm asking now, I want to talk about—

GUS

We've talked. We understand each other. You choose to live: Good, I want you to. But Jesus Christ, what life do you dream you're living? *(cont'd below:)*

EMPTY

I'm not dreaming anything, I—

GUS *(cont'd from above)*

Everything, everything predicted, every anticipated horror, it's coming true, it's here, it's upon us now! Money's the, the air now and the weather and water and the only knowable, lovable thing. People live and die in miserable deprivation so a handful of pigs in human shapes can inhabit their hollow heaven of valueless shit, and no one fights back because no one knows how anymore. And you want to keep me alive? What for?! To be a, an audience for *that*? *In what world do you dream you live?*

                    EMPTY *(a beat, then, suddenly afraid)*
Why am I here?

                    GUS *(pulling the anger back but it's still
                         there, only colder)*
The person I love most in the world. I need you here.

                    EMPTY
To, to *watch*? Why? You want your blood on my hands?

                    GUS
You think your hands are clean? And if they are, you're proud of that?

                    EMPTY
I'm not proud of, of anything, I'm ashamed that I let you, um, trick me into staying. You tricked me. I'm ashamed of you. *Coward. You coward.*

                    GUS
You watch the world dying and you find it bearable, but you can't bear the thought of, of what? What's so fucking scary? I'll tell you what: It's me showing you you're wrong that nothing's ever worth dying for, that's what you can't—

                    EMPTY
Stop it!! Stop it!! This isn't about who is or isn't watching, *it's not a fucking play*!! This is about actual, actual *blood*, or, or no, there's no blood this time, right? Just— *(gesturing toward the shopping bag)* Just, just—

GUS

Escape.

EMPTY

Obliteration. You escape, maybe, but your body, your *dead body* will be *here*, in this house, with me. You did this, this whole year, just to leave me alone with *that*? You ask me to dignify this . . . self-slaughter with political purpose, like your corpse makes some dream come true, your stupid meaningless death makes the revolution real, while surviving, going on living, that's play-acting. *No. NO.* You betray politics by doing this, by doing this you act to end all possibility of acting, of action, you cut yourself off from us, from life, from meaning. It doesn't matter if I'm watching or not, when you—*if* you kill yourself you choose to be alone and *that choice*, that's *despair.* That's cowardice. It's, it's hate. I think, I think you must . . . hate me, you want—

GUS

You know that's not true.

EMPTY

—you want to hurt me, to punish me for believing you, for believing in you, you want to punish yourself for lying and me for believing you that the world actually, um, *changed*, um, yielded— You want to destroy the miserable treacherous soft thing you think you've made of me.
(a pause)
Is it that? Am I right? Is that what you—

GUS

Yeah. Maybe.
The person I love most in the world is the person I want most to undo.
Maybe so.

(She stares at him. He reaches for her hand. She pulls her hand out of reach.)

GUS

Don't be scared, honey. I shouldn't've said that. I didn't mean it. *(cont'd below:)*

EMPTY

Okay, it's okay, I . . . I know that, I guess— *(cont'd below:)*

GUS *(cont'd from above)*

I can't think anymore. *(cont'd below:)*

EMPTY *(cont'd from above)*

Let's just get through tonight, okay? Alive. *(cont'd below:)*

GUS *(cont'd from above)*

I don't know how to anymore.

EMPTY *(cont'd from above)*

We'll both be clearer after we've slept. Only promise me—

GUS *(rage, despair, agony)*

I CAN'T. DON'T ASK ME THAT!! *I DON'T WANT TO LIVE ANYMORE, EMPTY. LET GO.*

(Empty sits, stunned. Then, without standing:)

EMPTY

I'm going to the kitchen. I'm calling the, the . . .

GUS

You won't, sweetheart. You haven't, and you won't. Because all along you've understood something of what I mean. I raised you to.

(Gus stands, slowly.)

GUS

Go on, then. *(cont'd below:)*

EMPTY

Oh no. Oh no.

GUS *(cont'd from above)*

Leave. I can do it without you. Or, or call the cops, if that's what you—

EMPTY

Oh no oh no, oh please stop this, oh please Daddy stop doing this, stop it stop it . . . *(cont'd below:)*

GUS

Call the cops. Imprison me.

EMPTY *(cont'd from above, a wail)*

OHHHHHH GOD!

(She stands, an impulse to run, but she doesn't know where to go.)

EMPTY

What'll I do? What'll I do?

(Gus stands, runs to her, wraps her in a tight embrace, which she permits, for a moment, before she suddenly growls and shoves him away. Gus stumbles back, almost falling.
She goes to the ruined wall and pushes her face against it, away from him. He stands, helpless, lost, watching her.)

GUS

Come back, please come back to me.

241

(She stays at the wall, not facing him.)

EMPTY

This is inhuman, what you've done. You're a monster.

GUS

I'm not. You know I'm not.

EMPTY *(considers that; shrug; then)*

Allora sei un minotauro.
(turns to face him)
I'm not calling anyone. I can't judge you. I don't have the . . .
The perspective. An unimpeded view.
But.
If you murder my father, he takes the part of me he's kept for
himself with him.

GUS

Yeah. Maybe.

EMPTY

How can I not hate you. Whoever you are. I'll work to make
your life, your death, mean nothing to me. I will hate you forever. I don't want to, but I will.
Please believe that. That's what it costs.

*(Gus steps toward her. She takes a step back, away from him.
They freeze.)*

Scene Three

Eli is standing in the parlor doorway, in yesterday's clothes;
he's an exhausted mess, and very nervous. Gus is standing in
the parlor.
The suitcase is on the table, open. The shopping bag is next to it.
Eli takes a wallet out of his coat pocket.

ELI

He left his wallet. Could you just give it to him?
(he opens the wallet to show) Everything's there, there aren't
credit cards but I didn't . . . *(nervous laugh)* There weren't any
when I found it, a few bucks, all there, some old receipts, and
this *(he takes a laminated ID with a picture on it from the wal-*
let) old photo of him . . . his high school swim club ID I guess?

(He holds it out to Gus, who doesn't move to take it.)

GUS

He was a good swimmer.

ELI

I bet. Knife-like.

(Gus stares at Eli.)

ELI *(showing the back of the ID)*

It, um, had this address.
(He puts the ID back in the wallet. Looking at the floor.)
I wanted him to have it. And oh well see him, or, the outside of his . . . Where he grew up?
(He gets upset, then panic overwhelms him: shallow breaths, racing heart, hyper-adrenalated. As he struggles to control it:)
I took some crap that was supposed to make me sleep. Didn't. Keyed me up. Panic attack, maybe, I can't— Haven't slept in, but I don't like sleep, what's it accomplish, you know?

GUS

Its use is that it's of no use.

ELI

Yeah.
(he's getting his panic under control)
You remind me of Pill.
Sorry, I should . . . You want me to . . . ?

(Eli holds the wallet out toward Gus, who doesn't move to take it. Eli goes to the table, places the wallet on it, then looks at the suitcase.)

ELI

Going someplace?

(Protectively, Gus slides the suitcase toward himself, out of Eli's reach.)

GUS

My grandfather's.

ELI

It looks old.

GUS

Turn of the last century.

ELI

No doubt.

(Defying Gus, Eli looks inside. He points to a bundle of paper slips, tied with a string.)

ELI

Lottery tickets?

GUS

Not exactly.

(Eli reaches toward the suitcase, then stops.)

ELI

Can I . . . ?

(Gus shrugs. Eli takes out an old, yellowed booklet of about thirty pages. He opens it.)

GUS

Careful.

245

ELI

You speak Italian, right?

GUS

Via, vaffanculo, finocchio.

(Eli doesn't know the meaning of the words but he takes in the aggression, unflinchingly. He looks down at the cover, which he reads with his good ear for the sound of it.)

ELI

Il Manifesto del Partito Comunista.
(grins) Well I know what *that* means.

(Eli puts the booklet on the table.)

ELI

Your granddad too, huh? Goes way back, I guess.

GUS

Anarcho-communist. From Paterson, New Jersey. He moved from there in 1900. To here.

ELI

How come?

GUS

Complicated.

ELI

I bet.

(Gus looks at him, then:)

GUS

In 1900 a Paterson guy, Gaetano Bresci, an immigrant, he sailed
back to Italy—

ELI

La patria.

GUS

Uh . . . right.
With a revolver, and he shot the King of Italy. Three bullets, in
the chest. Dead. Umberto Uno. Who'd decorated a sonofabitch
general for firing a cannon into a crowd of people protesting
the high price of bread.
Bresci belonged to an anarchist circle in Paterson. Italian
immigrants, millworkers. No one knows this, but the members
of the circle bought Bresci's ticket back to Italy, they bought
him the gun, they raised money for his family.

(He takes the bundle of papers out of the suitcase.)

GUS

These are their pledges. This one—

*(He puts the pledges back in the suitcase and then carefully
removes the one on top. He hands it to Eli.)*

GUS

—is my grandfather's.

(As Eli is looking at the pledge:)

GUS

They pay you for sex?

(Eli looks at Gus. Then he carefully puts the pledge back in the suitcase. He sees something beneath the pledges.)

ELI

What's the music for?

GUS

Also, they were a choral society. Anarchist-communist choral society. They sang. The Garibaldi March.

(Eli holds up sheet music: "Va Pensiero" from Nabucco.*)*

ELI

Verdi.

GUS

What else?
(Singing softly:)
"Va, pensiero, sull'ali dorate;
Va, ti posa Da dada dada da da . . ."
They got scared, what if Bresci would talk under torture? So they skedaddled. Went their separate ways.
Bresci, when he was arrested, he said, "I didn't kill a man, I killed a principle."

ELI

Huh. That's . . . I don't know about that.

GUS

And my Grandfather Nicolao Marcantonio came to Brooklyn. To this house, to work on the waterfront. To save, to prosper. To own.

(Gus looks around the room, then he takes the sheet music from Eli, puts it back in the suitcase and closes it.
Eli picks up the booklet from the tabletop.)

ELI

You left this.

GUS

Keep it.

ELI

Oh. Uh, thanks . . . ?

GUS

Maybe you oughta . . . *(go)*

ELI *(reading the first line of the first page
of the booklet)*

"Uno spettro si aggira—" *(he pronounces the "gg" as a hard "g")*

GUS *(correcting his pronunciation)*

"Aggira." Means "haunting." "Spettro" is a specter. A ghost.

ELI

A ghost? Like a, like a dead—

GUS *(reciting from memory)*

"La storia di ogni società sinora esistita è la storia di lotte di
classe."
"The story of all societies that have hitherto existed is the story
of class struggles."

*(Eli closes the booklet, looks up at Gus; then, reaching for the
shopping bag:)*

ELI

What's in there?

*(Gus snatches the bag away from Eli and holds it close, rolling
the top shut.)*

GUS

I don't know.

ELI *(a slow nod; then)*

You gonna—

GUS

How much do they pay you?

(Eli looks at him.)

GUS

By the hour?

ELI

Three hundred bucks.

GUS

Huh!
What does money like that buy?

(A beat. Then:)

ELI

It's complicated.

GUS

Yeah.

ELI

Kind of depends on your, um . . .

GUS

Perspective.

ELI

Right. Money buys you . . . Pretty much anything, Gus.
It's like . . . What do you want.

GUS

Right.

(They look at one another.)

ELI

So . . .
What do you want, Gus?

(Gus looks at the shopping bag he's holding, then at the suit-case; a beat, then:)

GUS

I'm thinking.

END OF PLAY

APPENDIX

CHRONOLOGY

1854 Peppino Marcantonio, born 1831 (?) in the town of Picerno, in the Basilicata region of southern Italy, marries Edmia Ismailla Viglongo, also born in Picerno, 1833 (?).

1855 Peppino and Edmia have a son, Ugo.

1860 Peppino and Edmia's second son, GioMaria, is born.

1875 Ugo marries Battista Marcias (birthdate and place unknown) and the couple emigrates to America, first to Manhattan, then settling in Cornwall-on-Hudson.

1877 GioMaria marries Grazia Sotgiu (born Sardinia, 1863). Their son Nicolao Marcantonio is born six months later, in Picerno.

1880 Ugo and Battista's son, Sanario, is born in Cornwall-on-Hudson, New York.

1892 Nicolao marries Maria Teresa Lusso (born 1872 in Picerno). They emigrate to America, settling in Paterson, New Jersey. Nicolao works in a textile factory, and joins a choral society of Italian immigrants that's also, secretly, an anarchist circle. Nicolao becomes a fervent anarcho-communist.

1900 Ugo and his son Sanario travel back to Picerno where Sanario is engaged to a cousin, Angelina DeDobitis (born Picerno, Italia, 1882). Ugo, Sanario and Angelina return to Cornwall-on-Hudson.

Gaetano Bresci, a textile worker from Paterson, NJ, travels back to Italy, his steerage-class ticket and revolver paid for by Nicolao's anarcho-communist circle, of which Bresci is a member. Upon arrival, Bresci assassinates Umberto I, the King of Italy, as a protest against the Italian army's slaughter of people demonstrating against the unaffordable price of basic foods, and to call the world's attention to the wrongful imprisonment, torture and murder of anarchists in Umberto's dungeons. After the assassination, fearing discovery of their part in the plot, the Paterson choral society/anarchist circle dissolves itself, and its members scatter. Nicolao moves his family to Carroll Gardens, a working-class Italian immigrant enclave in Brooklyn. They rent a small room on the second floor of a crowded brownstone, home to several Italian immigrant families.

1901 Sanario and Angelina move to East 112th Street, Manhattan. Nicolao becomes a stevedore on the Brooklyn waterfront, unloading cargo. He moves his family to south Brooklyn.

1902 Sanario and Angelina have a son, (future congressman) Vito Marcantonio.

1907 Gus and Clio's father, Matteo, is born to Nicolao and Maria in the brownstone on Clinton Street, in what will eventually be called Carroll Gardens.

1920 Sacco and Vanzetti, poor Italian immigrant workers and anarchists, are arrested in Brockton, Massachusetts.

1927 After two rigged trials, Sacco and Vanzetti are executed. They become martyrs but their judicial murder convinces many on the Left that anarchism's inherent disorganization and its egoistic romanticism is fatal to its revolutionary political efficacy.

1930 Matteo, a teamster now, working on the waterfront and a member of the International Longshoreman's Union, marries a Carroll Gardens woman, Rosa Iginia Torrefranca, a devout Catholic. Matteo has abandoned his father's anarcho-communist politics and since 1929 he's been a member of the American Communist Party (CPUSA).

1935 Gus (Augusto Giuseppe Garibaldi Marcantonio) is born.

1938 Clio (Clio Annunziata Marcantonio) is born.

1940 Taking advantage of a bank foreclosure, with money carefully saved and pooled together with another family's savings, Nicolao becomes part owner, and then owner of the brownstone.

1948 Gus works as a volunteer in the East Harlem offices of the American Labor Party for the reelection, to his sixth term in the U.S. House of Representatives, of his famous radical cousin, Vito Marcantonio.

1950 The Korean War begins. Vito Marcantonio, targeted for his refusal to vote for America's entry into the Korean War, is finally defeated by a coalition of New York's Democrat and Republican clubs and the gerrymandering of his district. Gus works on this campaign and spends time with Vito.

1951 Gus finishes high school one year early and becomes an apprentice teamster on the Brooklyn waterfront.

1952 Gus becomes a member of ILWU, the International Longshore and Warehouse Union, Local 1814. He then applies for membership in the CPUSA.

1953 Gus marries Claudia Magrini, a young woman from the neighborhood, religious like his mother, though of course more modern, and five years older than Gus. She's pregnant when he marries her.

After Eisenhower rescinds the paternity deferment for conscription, Gus receives his draft notice. He refuses to serve. He goes to federal prison at Leavenworth just as the Korean War comes to a close.

1954 Pill (PierLuigi Marcantonio) is born while Gus is in prison. Clio finishes high school and immediately, to her mother's delight and her father's and brother's horror, becomes a postulant with the Discalced Carmelites in Weehawken, New Jersey.

On his way to a printer to get posters made announcing his bid to return to Congress, Vito Marcantonio drops dead from a heart attack outside City Hall. Cardinal Spellman refuses to allow him to be given a Catholic burial. W. E. B. DuBois and Paul Robeson speak at his funeral; tens of thousands attend.

1955 Gus gets out of prison. He returns to the waterfront and his life as a teamster; he becomes deeply involved in union organizing and politics, serving on negotiating committees as a rank-and-file member, always refusing to hold elective office.

Clio becomes a novice with the Discalced Carmelites in Mexico City.

1956 On Feb 14–26, at the 20th Congress of the Communist Party of the Soviet Union in Moscow, Khrushchev denounces Stalin's crimes, causing earthquakes in communist parties around the world. Many leave, disillusioned. Gus doesn't.

1958 Empty (Maria Theresa Marcantonio) is born.

1959 Clio takes her solemn vows and becomes a Discalced Carmelite nun.

1965 Nicolao Marcantonio dies.

1968 On June 6, Claudia, who is now thirty-eight years old, gives birth to V (Vito Anthony Marcantonio). The pregnancy is a complicated one; in the third trimester the fetus starts bleeding and Claudia is confined to bed. Then following a long and difficult delivery, Claudia has difficulty releasing the placenta, causing a massive obstetric hemorrhage. This results in deep vein thrombosis, which is undiagnosed. Later that night, Claudia dies of a pulmonary embolism.

1969 Clio goes to a Carmelite convent in Lima, Peru. She becomes a devotee of St. Teresa of the Andes, inspired by the saint's writings, her life of poverty and devotion to the indigenous poor.

1971 Rosa Marcantonio dies.

1972 Facing containerization of the Brooklyn waterfront and the loss of jobs to automation, the ILWU goes out on strike.

Pill goes to University of Michigan at Ann Arbor for his undergraduate studies.

1973 After a long, bitter fight, the ILWU succeeds in securing a concession from the shipping and storage companies: A guaranteed annual income (GAI) for its senior membership, Gus among them. For the rest of their lives, those who receive the GAI will be paid whether or not there's work to do.

1974 The companies on the waterfront begin laying off the junior members of the ILWU. Gus and other men on the GAI, who've been working intermittently, find ways to avoid coming to work, at first to force the companies to employ more men, and then increasingly out of anger and disgust. Some stop reporting simply because they find other pursuits, or time with their families, or leisure more enticing than working the docks.

1975 Maria Theresa Marcantonio, Empty's great-grandmother and namesake, dies.

1976 Empty starts undergraduate studies at Hunter College.

Pill goes to Harvard for graduate work in U.S. history, specializing in labor history.

Gus begins doing voluntary or occasionally off-the-books paid work organizing for the ILWU, which is trying now to organize non-waterfront warehouse workers.

1978 Pill gets his master's degree, begins work on his doctoral dissertation on the San Francisco ILU strike of 1935.

1980 Empty graduates and goes straight to medical school at Cornell.

1981 Pill meets Paul while Paul is a sophomore at Harvard and Pill continues to work on his dissertation.

1983 Empty drops out of med school.

1984 Empty goes into a nursing program for two years.

1985 V graduates from high school. He enrolls in Brooklyn College.

Clio, still a Carmelite nun but having abandoned the order's charism of contemplation and seclusion, is doing poverty work in an Andean village that's overtaken and held for nearly two years by Maoist guerrillas, either of the Tupac Amaru Army or the more dangerous Sendero Luminuso (the Shining Path).

1986 Empty works as a nurse for six years, a member of 1199, the nurses' union.

V drops out of Brooklyn College. He apprentices with the ILWU for work on the waterfront and waits all year to be hired.

1987 V leaves the ILWU and apprentices with the United Brothers of Carpenters, Local 926.

Clio leaves her order and the Church, and forges a shadowy, extremely risky connection with armed Andean resistance groups, for a time following the Maoist line of Sendero Luminoso's chief, Commander Gonzo. She continues to live in various locations in the foothills of the Andes; she's an infrequent and, during this period, alarming visitor to Gus's home in Brooklyn.

1989 V becomes a member of the Carpenters' Local 926.

Gus does voluntary organizing work for the Printing Trades Council in preparation for a strike at the *Daily News*.

1990 Gus spends five months supporting the striking *Daily News* workers. Empty also volunteers extensively through 1199, which supports the strike.

1991 Paul graduates from Harvard Divinity with a ThD. Pill is still working on his dissertation and is teaching high school in Boston. Later that year, Paul gets a postdoc fellowship at NYU's Humanities Institute. They move to New York, Pill teaches high school in Washington Heights.

The *Daily News* strike ends when British billionaire Robert Maxwell makes an offer to buy the paper.

The Cleveland Convention of the CPUSA, where dissenters from the Executive's decision to support the coup attempt against Gorbachev, form the Commie Dissident Committees of Correspondence. Later that year, Gus leaves the CPUSA, joining with the CofC. He does organizing work for them.

Robert Maxwell falls off his yacht and drowns; the *Daily News* deal falls apart and the newspaper enters Chapter 11 bankruptcy.

Matteo Marcantonio dies.

Clio returns to the U.S., living in various places around New York City. She half-heartedly joins a Maoist group, the Revolutionary Communist Party.

1992 Empty, having become interested in labor law through 1199's political activities, leaves nursing.

1994 Empty attends Cardozo Law School in Manhattan.

Clio leaves the RCP and moves to a public housing project in Paterson, New Jersey.

1995 Gus becomes inactive in the CofC and begins to teach himself Latin.

1996 Paul, now an Assistant Professor in the Comparative Religion Dept at NYU, is offered a tenure track Assistant Professorship of Theology at Union Theological Seminary/Columbia University.

1997 Empty meets Adam in the spring of their last year of law school. They graduate in May. Immediately upon graduation, Empty goes to work in the legal department at 1199. In the fall, Adam becomes licensed real-estate lawyer.

1998 V meets Sooze Lim, age twenty-four, in the neighborhood. She works as an accountant in a Wall Street firm.

Empty and Adam get married.

2000 V and Sooze get married.

2001 Maeve begins graduate studies at Union Theological Seminary at age thirty-four.

Paul makes Associate Professor, becomes Maeve's thesis advisor.

V starts his own contracting business. Sooze handles the bookkeeping.

2002 Early in the year, Gus rejoins the Communist Party.

Empty goes to work at a foundation that supports the advancement of trade unionism and labor law. She specializes in domestic labor organizing and works on the drafting of and legislative campaign for what will become EFCA, the Employee Free Choice Act.

Pill makes an effort to reshape his old dissertation. His extramarital and expensive sexual activities begin to consume more and more of his time. He deems the dissertation unfixable.

Pill and Paul throw a party at which Empty meets Maeve. They fall in love.

2003 Empty divorces Adam. Maeve moves into Empty's (and formerly Adam's) apartment while Adam moves to the garden apartment of the brownstone in Carroll Gardens, invited by Gus.

2004 Alice Marcantonio is born to V and Sooze, who quits her Wall Street job to devote herself to her baby, and to helping V run his prospering business, which now employs two crews of men.

Maeve, nearing completion of her class work and preparing to work on her dissertation, tells Empty she wants to have a baby, soon. Empty considers, and refuses. She has no interest in having children. They argue. Maeve wins. They establish a joint bank account to pay for insemination when Maeve completes her dissertation.

Paul publishes a lauded (within academic circles) book: *On Systematic Theology: Dispensationalism and African-American Political Trajectories in the American South.*

2005 Gus retires and begins to receive his small GAI pension, having spent fifty-four years as a longshoreman, and thirty-two years not working on the waterfront.

In January, Paul learns he will be up for full tenure in the 2005–2006 academic year.

In February, Pill, cruising on the internet, finds Eli's ad on Craigslist. By midyear, Pill starts to borrow money from Empty to pay for the time he's spending with Eli, eventually borrowing more than thirty thousand dollars.

2006 In January, Maeve completes the first draft of her dissertation, a perhaps overly ambitious survey of apophatic-docetic Christologies, the hypophatic union, kenosis, Dionysius the Pseudo-Areopagite and the Dialexia de Non-Certitudine of Juan Caramuel y Lobkowitz.

In February, V and Sooze have a baby boy, Leo.

In March, Maeve decides that, while she refines her diss in preparation for its defense, she wants to start insemination. She discovers that the insemination fund is empty. She confronts Empty, who confesses that she's loaned all the money to Pill. Maeve tells Paul. Paul confronts Pill and then, when Pill refuses to stop the affair, Paul threatens Eli.

From April–May, Maeve and Empty fight about Maeve's telling Paul. Empty refuses to sleep with Maeve. Since they can no longer afford to go to a clinic for insemination, Maeve insists on getting Vito's sperm and using a turkey baster. Empty consents, very reluctantly. Maeve gets sperm donations from V, but without success.

Paul convinces Pill to leave New York and Eli, and to enter a program to deal with his sex addiction, including his compulsive solicitation of hustlers. Paul applies for and is accepted for an assistant professorship at University of Minnesota in Minneapolis, a joint appointment of the African-American Studies Department, the Religious Studies Department, and the Department of Gender, Women and Sexuality Studies.

In May, after the semester at Columbia ends, Pill and Paul move to Minneapolis. Shortly after arriving, Pill, through cell phone and email, resumes contact with Eli.

On June 6, V's birthday, Gus slashes his wrists in the bathtub. He's found, naked, in the garden, by Adam, who calls 911, then Empty and V. Gus is taken to King's County Hospital, V and Adam accompanying. Empty meets them at the hospital. Gus is put on a locked ward and heavily sedated. Pill and Paul are contacted in Minneapolis. Pill stays put. Gus spends three weeks on the locked ward.

In July, On his doctors' advice, to expedite his release, which Empty is facilitating, Gus asks Clio to move in for a while. She does.

Maeve and Empty (mostly Maeve) begin routine visits to V and Sooze's Carroll Gardens apartment to collect V's semen.

By November, Maeve is making her semen-collecting trips to Brooklyn alone, Empty having dropped out of the process. Maeve finds V at home, Sooze out for the evening, the kids asleep; Maeve and V have sex.

In December, Maeve learns that she's pregnant.

Around Christmas, Eli's increasingly intermittent contact with Pill ceases altogether; he becomes unreachable.

2007 In March, Gus meets Shelle in a bar.

Gus asks Adam to help him find a buyer for the brownstone.

Paul returns to New York to take part in Maeve's dissertation defense. In spite of his hostile questioning during her oral defense, the dissertation is accepted by the committee.

In May, Gus starts burning his papers. Clio calls Empty.

Adam tells Gus that he has a buyer with a four-million-dollar offer.

On June 10, Gus tells Clio that he's decided to commit suicide. Clio calls the kids.

Pill's emails to Eli have gone unanswered for months. Now Pill writes to say he'll be returning to New York, explaining for the first time that his father is suicidal. Eli replies in an email full of questions about Gus's suicide attempt and threat.

On June 15, the play begins.

GUS'S TRANSLATION OF HORACE'S EPISTLE XVI

Gus makes reference to two of Horace's epistles. Epistle II, Book Two, contains the passage about the citizen of Argos discussed in Act Two, Scene One. Gus has completed this translation more than a year before the play begins.

During the play, Gus is finishing his translation of Horace's Epistle XVI, Book One; this epistle contains a prayer to the Goddess of Falsehoods, Laverna (Lauerna in Latin), which Gus tries to recite for V in Act Three. Below is the Latin original of Epistle XVI, followed by Gus's translation.

THE EPISTLES OF HORACE, BOOK ONE, EPISTLE XVI

1 Ne perconteris, fundus meus, optime Quincti,
aruo pascat erum an bacis opulentet oliuae,
pomisne et pratis an amicta uitibus ulmo,
scribetur tibi forma loquaciter et situs agri.
Continui montes, ni dissocientur opaca
ualle, sed ut ueniens dextrum latus aspiciat sol,
laeuum discedens curru fugiente uaporet.
2 Temperiem laudes. Quid, si rubicunda benigni
corna uepres et pruna ferant, si quercus et ilex
multa fruge pecus, multa dominum iuuet umbra?
Dicas adductum propius frondere Tarentum.
Fons etiam riuo dare nomen idoneus, ut nec

frigidior Thraecam nec purior ambiat Hebrus,
infirmo capiti fluit utilis, utilis aluo.

3 Hae latebrae dulces et, iam si credis, amoenae
incolumem tibi me praestant septembribus horis.
Tu recte uiuis, si curas esse quod audis.
Iactamus iampridem omnis te Roma beatum;
sed uereor, ne cui de te plus quam tibi credas
neue putes alium sapiente bonoque beatum,
neu, si te populus sanum recteque ualentem
dictitet, occultam febrem sub tempus edendi
dissimules, donec manibus tremor incidat unctis.

4 Stultorum incurata pudor malus ulcera celat.
Siquis bella tibi terra pugnata marique
dicat et his uerbis uacuas permulceat auris:
'Tene magis saluum populus uelit an populum tu,
seruet in ambiguo qui consulit et tibi et urbi
Iuppiter', Augusti laudes adgnoscere possis;
cum pateris sapiens emendatusque uocari,
respondesne tuo, dic sodes, nomine?

5   'Nempe
uir bonus et prudens dici delector ego ac tu.'
Qui dedit hoc hodie, cras si uolet auferet, ut, si
detulerit fasces indigno, detrahet idem.
Pone, meum est,' inquit; pono tristisque recedo.
Idem si clamet furem, neget esse pudicum,
contendat laqueo collum pressisse paternum,
mordear opprobriis falsis mutemque colores?
Falsus honor iuuat et mendax infamia terret
quem nisi mendosum et medicandum? Vir bonus est quis?

6 'Qui consulta patrum, qui leges iuraque seruat,
quo multae magnaeque secantur iudice lites,
quo res sponsore et quo causae teste tenentur.'
Sed uidet hunc omnis domus et uicinia tota
introrsum turpem, speciosum pelle decora.
'Nec furtum feci nec fugi,' si mihi dicat
seruos: 'Habes pretium, loris non ureris', aio.

'Non hominem occidi.' 'Non pasces in cruce coruos.'
'Sum bonus et frugi.' Renuit negitatque Sabellus.
7 Cautus enim metuit foueam lupus accipiterque
suspectos laqueos et opertum miluus hamum.
Oderunt peccare boni uirtutis amore;
tu nihil admittes in te formidine poenae;
sit spes fallendi, miscebis sacra profanis.
Nam de mille fabae modiis cum subripis unum,
damnum est, non facinus mihi pacto lenius isto.
Vir bonus, omne forum quem spectat et omne tribunal,
quandocumque deos uel porco uel boue placat:
'Iane pater!' clare, clare cum dixit: 'Apollo!'
labra mouet, metuens audiri:
8   'Pulchra Lauerna,
da mihi fallere, da iusto sanctoque uideri,
noctem peccatis et fraudibus obice nubem.'
Qui melior seruo, qui liberior sit auarus,
in triuiis fixum cum se demittit ob assem,
non uideo; nam qui cupiet, metuet quoque, porro
qui metuens uiuet, liber mihi non erit umquam.
Perdidit arma, locum uirtutis deseruit, qui
semper in augenda festinat et obruitur re.
Vendere cum possis captiuum, occidere noli;
seruiet utiliter; sine pascat durus aretque,
nauiget ac mediis hiemet mercator in undis,
annonae prosit, portet frumenta penusque.
9 Vir bonus et sapiens audebit dicere: 'Pentheu,
rector Thebarum, quid me perferre patique
indignum coges?' 'Adimam bona.' 'Nempe pecus, rem,
lectos, argentum; tollas licet.' 'In manicis et
compedibus saeuo te sub custode tenebo.'
'Ipse deus, simul atque uolam, me soluet.' Opinor,
hoc sentit: 'Moriar'. Mors ultima linea rerum est.

The Epistles of Horace, Book One, Epistle XVI

Translated from the Latin by Gus Marcantonio, Local 1814
International Longshore and Warehouse Union (retired).
Carroll Gardens, Brooklyn. May–June 2007.

1 Dear Quinctius, Don't worry about my farm,
if there are cornfields, if the olive crops make me rich,
what's up with my orchards, pastures,
whether vines wrap around the elm trees.
I'll go on and on covering every detail, writing to you.
Surrounded by mountains, the valley's shadowed;
when the sun rises his aspect is of the right side,
and as he's fleeing, of the left.
2   You'd love the climate.
How could you feel otherwise, when the thornbushes
make sweet red berries, and plums for prunes,
and the oaks make acorns for the cattle, and
for the owner of all of this, they make shade?
You'd say that it's like leafy Tarentum was suddenly
more accessible. There's a spring,
worthy of the river it's named after,
as cooling and refreshing as the Hebrus is to Thrace,
the flowing of which has use-value to the unwell mind,
useful to the guts as well.
3 It's thanks to this sweet and, please believe me, wondrous hideaway
that I present myself to you, pickled in good health, even in autumn.
You're rectitudinous, if careful of your reputation.
For many years Rome's praised you as happy.
But I'm worried that you might believe what others say about you,
or that you'll believe you can be happy without being wise and good,
or, just because people say you're healthy and upstanding,
you'll hide that palsy you often get at suppertime,
concealing your greasy, shaky hands.

4 Only a ~~fool~~ moron denies out of pride that he's got ulcers.
When they go on about the battles you've fought,
on land and sea, and catch your attention
saying things like "Jupiter, who watches over you and the city,
keeps it unclear who cares more for the other, you or the city,"
praise that, as you know, is really only fit for Augustus,
when they tell you you're a philosopher
and a man of distinguished tastes,
do you recognize yourself in all that?
5 I'd love it if they spoke of me that way, wise and good.
Who wouldn't? But they build you up today
to knock you ~~down~~ flat tomorrow, they make you a ~~big shot~~ consul
just so they can ~~sack dismiss~~ fire you: "It's up to us!"
they announce: "Get lost!" Cut down to size, I retire, pronto.
And thus, when they say that I'm a jerk, say I can't control myself,
say that I strangled my father with a horse-bridle,
does this upset me, do I blush because they smear?
Who enjoys undeserved praise, who's frightened by slander?
Phonies and weaklings. So then, a good man – who is he?
6 The one who ~~consults~~ ~~pays attention to~~ ~~obeys~~ consults those he
elects,
who's law-abiding, just, settles arguments, stakes claims,
and testifies for causes he believes in.
But maybe this man's household and his neighbors notice
that his decorous manner's a flimsy front, rotten inside.
"I've never stolen from you, I've never been a runaway!"
If my slave tells me that, I respond "Here, have your reward: I've never
beaten you for doing so." He says "I didn't murder either."
"Then you won't end up crow-food on a crucifix." He says
"I am a frugal, righteous man!" This common farmer shakes his head
    at that, dubious.
7 The cautious wolf sidesteps the wolftrap, the hawk's suspicious of
    snares,
the pike slips past the baited hook; the good man despises evil.
You do good because you're afraid of getting caught.

If you could get away with it, you'd be holy one minute, profane the
 next.
If you steal only one of my thousands of bushels of beans,
my loss is a little thing, but your wickedness isn't.
A good man like you, respected in the marketplace, revered in the
 law courts,
sacrifices a pig or an ox to the gods, calling 'Janus Father!'
in a clear, clear voice, 'Apollo!' But you barely move your lips,
afraid you might be heard, when you also pray
8   'O lovely Laverna,
make me a good liar, make me seem righteous and just,
let night cover my sins and thick clouds obscure my fraudulence!'"
Is a free miser any better than a slave if every penny he sees
dropped in the road makes him bow down to pick it up?
To be envious is to be anxious, and anxious men, I think,
aren't free. Rushing about, frantic to get richer,
they drop their weapons and abandon their posts
as defenders of virtue. If you capture men who act this way,
don't kill them; enslave them and sell them. You can make a profit.
Or put them to work, feeding your livestock or plowing; sailing ships
in winter; trading corn and dry goods in the market;
they're ~~oxen~~ drudges ~~pack animals~~, they're used to drudgery.
9 The good man, the wise man is brave enough to say,
as the disguised god said in Euripides's play *The Bacchae:*
"Pentheus, king of Thebes, what terrible things can you do to me?"
"I'll take everything you have." "My cattle, you mean? My farm,
my possessions and bank account? Take them." "And I'll shackle you
hand and foot, and hand you over to a sadistic jailer." "God will free me,
as soon as I ask him to." What the character's saying is: "I'll die."
That's my understanding. The last line always belongs to death.

PLAYWRIGHT'S NOTES

A Note for Actors and Directors

Dear Actors and Directors:

The structure of the scenes in which there's extensive overlapping dialogue depends on strictly adhering to the stage directions that tell you when to continue speaking below, continue speaking from above, and when to speak over the line above your line. Every actor has to obey these directions, or the scene will fall apart. You must know *exactly* when to start speaking, and by what point you should be finished speaking. No exceptions, and no improvising.

If these directions are strictly adhered to, if these scenes are played with precision, I promise you they'll work. If the directions are ignored, or treated casually, the overlapping dialogue will be unplayable and incomprehensible to the audience.

The illusion of chaos is of course very different from actual chaos. If the overlapping dialogue is played as written, there will be moments when the audience has to choose which of several simultaneous exchanges to listen to, and other moments when it's possible for them to hear several arguments at once and comprehend what's important in each of them. When the entire audience is meant to focus on a single exchange or a single character, the chaos onstage will resolve/recede to permit that—again, provided that the stage directions are strictly adhered to. Those moments, when the audience realizes that the chaos is carefully orchestrated, are really worth the effort it takes to play the scenes with precision and care.

Many actors lower their voices, out of courtesy, when speaking at the same time as other actors. And some directors attempt to control which lines the audience hears, when there's simultaneous speaking onstage, by asking some actors to speak more or less quietly. Please don't do this! Speak as you normally would, at a volume appropriate to the action you're playing. While courtesy is always commendable, if you speak quietly while someone else is speaking normally, your lines, most likely unintelligible, will still be audible as meaningless murmuring. You'll only make it difficult for the audience to hear and/or focus on the actors who are speaking normally. If everyone speaks at a normal volume while overlapping, it's possible for the audience to follow whomever and whatever they choose to listen to; realizing this, they work hard to catch as much as they can and make choices when they must.

A Short Note Concerning Gus and a Long Note Concerning Clio

FOR ACTORS PLAYING GUS

On page 127, Gus says "cockaroaches," which is pronounced "cock-uh-roaches." I mention it because actors often read it as "cockroaches," omitting the extra syllable. Please don't omit it. It's a Brooklyn thing.

FOR ACTRESSES PLAYING CLIO

Clio has been through a lot. She's had a long and difficult life. She's witnessed terrible things. She's been contiguous to, and complicit in terrible crimes; the extent of that complicity is something she keeps to herself. A demon inside her was set loose, and Clio's had to exercise fierce discipline, to practice withdrawal and self-abnegation in order to force it back into its cave. Clio harbors no illusions that the demon is dead, merely imprisoned, and she's devoted herself to serving as its vigilant warden.

Her suffering, her disillusionments and her guilt have not led Clio into despair, nor has she renounced her dedication to justice and equality, her determination to be of use, to be of help, to do good in the world. She's fought her way back to sanity, and to a new kind of service, delimited by immediacy, practicality, modesty of scale and ambition—in other words, she's found a kind of realism, shorn of grand theological or political theory.

Having no theory, no sacred text to guide her, Clio has abandoned proselytizing. Her advice, when it's requested, is given carefully and never insisted upon. Clio is thoroughly present in any gathering she chooses to attend, in any community in which she has a place or with which she finds an affinity. But she's learned how to be present and participate primarily by listening. She speaks only when she's certain that she has something of value to contribute.

To all her interactions with others, Clio brings a deep, hard-won understanding of the nature of power and of force; she has grappled all her life with the difference between the two and the limitations of both. She doesn't make the common mistake of confusing either power or force with rhetoric, emotionality or volume. She's not superhuman, not a bodhisattva; she's worked hard to give up judging. She engages in an internal struggle to adhere faithfully to her newfound catechism without lapsing into zealotry.

I think that an actress playing Clio will know she's gotten close to the character when she feels she's doing almost nothing. Clio feels deeply, loves deeply, is curious, witty, angry, sad. But she doesn't allow herself the freedom of expression that everyone else assumes is unquestionably theirs. Clio opts instead for discipline, trusting that it'll make her as effective as it's possible to be, while acknowledging to herself, and to others when necessary, that there are hard limits to one's effectivity. Clio walks the line.

She isn't soft-spoken; when she decides to speak she's decided to be heard, and so her voice is clear and as strong as needed to be heard by anyone who wants to listen. Unlike everyone else in the family, Clio never shouts.

It's probably a little counterintuitive for an actor to trust that if she plays someone so self-contained, private, and indifferent to attention, she won't be boring or in danger of disappearing. But in the Marcantonio brownstone, everyone else is an epic talker and a ferocious fighter. Clio's stillness and reserve are riveting, unnerving; she manifests an alternative to what's usually identified as power, and in doing so reveals a clarity and strength the other characters don't possess. Clio becomes central to the play through her refusal to compete for center stage.

A Note About the Singing

In Act One, Scene Four, Eli sings "Pensa che un popolo" from Act Three of *Aida*; in Act Four, Scene One, Shelle and Gus sing a few lines of Woody Guthrie's "There Once Was a Union Maid"; and in Act Four, Scene Three, Gus sings the opening of "Va pensiero" from Act Three of *Nabucco*.

In 2016, Michael Friedman, *iHo*'s original composer, recorded mp4 files for the use of actors who play these characters. The files are available online:

https://www.heatandlightcoinc.com/ihomusic

Regarding these files, Michael made one mistake: On "Union Maid," he makes "sheriff" and "raid" plural: "the deputy sheriffs who made the raids." The correct lyrics are: "the deputy sheriff who made the raid." Otherwise, his versions are perfect, and it's a chance to hear the voice of Michael Friedman, which is perfect heaven. What we lost when we lost him is incalculable and imponderable.

Act One, Scene Four: Pre-Scene

Lots of scenes in this play begin with the action already underway; events that precede the onstage action will be inferred in what unfolds. Immediately before Act One, Scene Four commences, Pill has arrived at Eli's room and they've made an agreement, the nature of which determines the course of the scene, at least initially. Since I've found it useful, in production, to explain the specifics of their arrangement, I decided to turn my explanation into the pre-scene below, which is intended only for informational purposes. If it's helpful to use it in rehearsals, that's great; but please don't perform it as part of the play. If the actors playing Pill and Eli understand what these lines contain, the audience won't need to hear them. And the last thing this play needs is additional length!

Pill and Eli are in Eli's small studio apartment—a single room, really, in a SRO, a sink but no bathroom—on West 48th Street between 8th and 9th Avenues in Manhattan. The room's largely taken up by Eli's bed, on which Eli is sitting. Pill's standing by the door.

                              ELI

Okay, three rules of engagement, or otherwise you can't stay.

(Pill nods.)

                              ELI

First, I charge three hundred dollars an hour.

                              PILL

Wow, that's . . . a thirty-three-percent increase.

                              ELI

Inflation. Whatever. No discounts.

                              PILL

Okay. Two hours, then.

                              ELI

Second rule: No sex.

                              PILL

For six hundred bucks?

                              ELI

You said on the phone you just wanted to talk, that's what you—

                              PILL

I know, but six hundred dollars, that's—

                              ELI

It's for two hours of my time. Pay up or fuck off.

                    PILL *(a beat, then)*

What's the third rule?

ELI

No talk about anything personal. No apologies or excuses for, for just disappearing on me, no questions about what I've been up to for the past year, none of the shit you kept emailing about, I don't— *(cont'd below:)*

PILL

That's— The whole point of coming over was to see how—

ELI *(cont'd from above)*

And none of your lectures about whatever you assume is my current, um, situation, which is like totally no longer any of your fucking beeswax. And you are *not* going to ramrod me into, into getting into shit that'll just, um, destabilize me so you can feel good about yourself when you go back to—

PILL

Okay, okay, I . . .
Okay. You're right. We'll keep it impersonal.
Can I blow you? Would that . . . ?

(Eli stares at him, not amused.
Pill takes out his wallet, takes out all the cash he has, and hands it to Eli. Eli hesitates, then takes the money.)

PILL

I thought it'd buy me three hours at least.
This is awkward. What are we going to talk about?

(Eli holds the money out to Pill, offering a refund.)

PILL

We can't pretend to be strangers.

ELI

Why? That's exactly what we are.

(Pill stares at him, then starts to lose it.)

ELI

Rule number four: No crying.

PILL *(wiping his eyes)*

Sorry, sorry, it's— Not just you, it's . . . everything, being back and—

ELI *(holding out the money)*

Yeah, but rule number three, I told you I don't—

PILL

I don't understand why you never answered any of my emails, or, or talk to me, you said you'd keep in touch with me, you promised me you would. *(cont'd below:)*

ELI

Yeah, I don't think you should scold other people about breaking promises, you're like the reigning Miss America of broken— *(cont'd below:)*

PILL *(cont'd from above)*

Were you, was that punishment or, or indifference or—

ELI *(cont'd from above, peeling a few bills from the wad Pill has handed him)*

I'm taking something from the six hundred dollars to, to compensate for the past however many minutes of my time you're wasting, and *here*:

(Eli stands and throws the rest of the cash at Pill.)

ELI

Now I mean it, Pill, take your money and get out of my apartment.

PILL

This is, this is a room, it's not an—

ELI

LEAVE.

PILL

I think you should worry a little at least about how comfortable
you seem to be with, with estrangement, this . . . rigidity, it's
not— I mean inflexibility isn't maturity, it's—

ELI

And now you're lecturing me. *(cont'd below:)*

PILL

No I'm not, I'm just making an observation, that— *(cont'd
below:)*

ELI *(cont'd from above)*

About maturity. Which is particularly like stomach-turning,
considering.

PILL

Sex work runs the risk of loss of self, same as any other kind
of alienated labor.

*(Eli stares at him, furious, not responding. Pill looks at the money
on the floor. Then he starts picking it up, talking as he does:)*

PILL

Relationships become, um, friable, mercantile, contractual—
Okay, it's a lecture, in thin theoretical disguise, but I think
it's—

*(He's gathered all the money. They stare at each other, in
silence, not knowing how to proceed. Then:)*

ELI

What's alienated labor?

PILL

What?

ELI

What is that? I don't know what it—

PILL

It's . . . I don't really feel like—

ELI

Then leave.

PILL *(a beat, then)*

It's— Jesus it's so basic, I can't remember how it— The theory
of alienation of labor, it's, like, it's—

ELI *(holds out his hand for the money)*

Three hundred dollars an hour.

(Pill considers this, then hands Eli the money.)

ELI

Two hours?

PILL

It's . . . a difficult concept.

ELI

It's your money. Go. Start. The theory of alienation is . . .

*(Eli starts slowly to count the money as Pill starts to explain.
Act One, Scene Four begins.)*

AFTERWORD AND ACKNOWLEDGMENTS

In 2005 I got a phone call from Joe Dowling in Minneapolis asking whether I'd be amenable to a festival of my work at the Guthrie Theater, of which Joe was artistic director. His plan was to produce two already existing plays of mine, one on the Guthrie's thrust stage and one in its black box studio, and to commission a new play for the large proscenium house. The festival would begin in the spring of 2009. I said yes, immediately and enthusiastically.

Before I knew much of what the new play would be about, I had a title for it, poached from George Bernard Shaw, as had been the subtitle of the previous play I'd written that focused on LGBTQ concerns. *A Gay Fantasia on National Themes*, the subtitle of *Angels in America*, was borrowed from Shaw's *Heartbreak House*, which was subtitled *A Fantasia in the Russian Manner on National Themes*. For my new play, I decided to appropriate the title of Shaw's 1928 book-length exegesis on

Fabian socialist principles, *The Intelligent Woman's Guide to Socialism and Capitalism.*

Or rather I reappropriated it. Years before, when I turned forty, I wrote a free-associative monologue called *The Intelligent Homosexual's Guide to Capitalism and Socialism with a Key to the Scriptures.* The final six words of that title are also related to *Angels*; in the 1980s, preparing to write it, as part of my research into home-grown American religions I read Mary Baker Eddy's *Science and Health with a Key to the Scriptures.*

In other words, without knowing what the play would be, I knew that whatever I wrote for the first time since *Angels* would revolve around queerness, specifically homosexuality. And more: There's the title's promise to guide intelligent homosexuals through the complexities of capitalism and socialism. For many years, I'd been accumulating thoughts and questions about the past and future of organized labor, labor unions, economic justice, and injustice. I'd long intended to write something about labor—which is to say, about capitalism and socialism—but I'd never figured out how. As I began to look around for a play that would fit my title, two things occurred that made me feel the time had come to write about it.

In 2007, the collective bargaining agreement expired between IATSE's Local One, the Broadway stagehands union, and the League of American Theaters and Producers. Local One threatened to go on strike. When negotiations broke down, the stagehands closed theaters and walked on picket lines. A few days later, negotiations resumed and eventually a settlement was reached.

It seemed to me that public support for the striking stagehands was muted, to say the least. The press reported that top-tier stagehands were earning around $1600 a week, more with overtime; that some of these stagehands owned substantial homes on Long Island; that Local One had a fund to help pay college tuitions for their members' children. This relative affluence, which seemed to me a success story of organized labor, was regarded by numerous colleagues and friends of mine as something aberrant, outrageous. They argued that the stagehands had seized an unfair share of theater's limited riches, that Local One had obtained economic security for its members at the expense of actors, directors, designers, and playwrights whose livelihoods were, for the most part, meager and wildly insecure. The producers' and theater owners' assertion that the salaries of backstage crews were responsible for Broadway's appallingly inflated ticket prices was met with agreement rather than skepticism.

But the greatest ire and contempt was reserved for the union's refusal to allow producers to reduce stage crews to whatever size they deemed necessary for each show. Local One was demanding a degree of guaranteed employment from the industry they helped to create and kept operating; producers would be forced to employ stagehands *even when there was no work to be performed*. To many, this demand, beyond all else, was brazenly, patently unfair, indefensible, insane. Why should management have to pay workers for not working?

But it seemed to me that at the heart of Local One's demands was a thrilling insistence that workers' lives are real, actual, human lives that can't be put on pause for the sake of maximizing profits. I thought that Local One was announcing, in defiance of the spirit and temper of our era of rampaging, unfettered oligarchs, that workers aren't expendable, that workers have an inviolable relationship to their place of work beyond the hours they clock in. The theater strike of 2007, short as it was, undramatic as its resolution was, was a battle over elemental relationships of time, work and money. All labor disputes, all efforts to organize workers, haul us, all of us, into a confrontation with fundamental, foundational truths and illusions.

Of course I didn't conduct a systematic survey of attitudes towards the Local One strike, and I don't mean to suggest that most people in New York City or in the theater community are unambivalent about capital logic, the assumptions about wealth, ownership, wages and profits on which capitalism is predicated. None of us is immune to that logic or those assumptions, and I certainly include myself among the infected. I spoke to many people who sided with the workers. But when the strike began, I'd expected from my crowd a more wholeheartedly enthusiastic pro-union consensus. Given the perennially shaky scarcity economy of the theater, that was probably unrealistic; maybe my enthusiasm owed something to having partly dodged the vicissitudes of that economy by making my living writing movies. However, all nuances and asterisks aside, it was my distinct impression at the time that the logic upon which the right of workers is predicated—the right to organize, to demand a share of the wealth their labor creates, to strike in order to compel owners and management to accede to their demands—appeared to have become alien, nonsensical, illogical, a lost, dead language to a surprisingly sizable number of people.

It was this strike, a New York strike, a theater strike, that fortified my resolve to write something about labor. But it was a book that gave me a story to tell. It's a study of the 1971 Brooklyn dockyards strike called *Longshoremen*. Its author is my friend, the late Bill DeFazio, a sociologist. Bill's particular focus was on the members of the International Longshoremens' Union who, as part of the settlement with the shipping companies, had received a guaranteed annual income. A number of the men in Bill's study had resided in Brooklyn's Carroll Gardens, an Italian-American working-class neighborhood in which I'd lived for thirteen years, from 1982–1995.

At the confluence of the Local One strike and Bill's book about the 1971 ILU strike, a story began to emerge about a working-class Italian-American family that owned a Carroll Gardens brownstone. I decided that this fictional family would be relatives of the real-life six-term radical-left U.S. Congressman Vito Marcantonio.

Years ago, in a 1940s photo of a street in Spanish Harlem, I noticed election posters for Vito Marcantonio plastered on a wall. I was intrigued by this handsome man with an Italian name who'd run for Congress in Spanish Harlem. He is a largely forgotten but formidable figure in the now largely overlooked but immensely significant history of Italian-American left-political activism. (Not forgotten by everyone: Edward Albee told me that he'd cast his first vote for Vito Marcantonio.)

I had no idea what labor and homosexuality and Vito Marcantonio's imaginary Carroll Garden relatives had to do with one another, but that didn't concern me much. My plays are usually constructed by burrowing down to find connections between disparate, apparently unrelated elements. It was only 2007, I still had two years to write the play. I'd burrow; I'd think of something.

The only obstacle I faced before really getting going on the play was the screenplay I was writing, an adaptation of Doris Kearns Goodwin's magisterial *Team of Rivals* for Steven Spielberg. In 2005, when I promised Joe Dowling a new play in time for the 2009 festival, I'd just begun work on the screenplay, which I'd reckoned would take two years to write. Those two years flew by, and I was still struggling with *Lincoln*, the end not remotely in sight. Meanwhile the Guthrie Theater had announced the festival, including the news that my new play with a very long title would open on May 22, 2009.

On the fateful day in 2005 when I said yes to Joe, I guess I was too excited to notice that in saying yes I was violating a cardinal rule of playwriting: Never ever ever agree to a date for the opening night of a play you haven't written yet.

As it happened, it took three years, not two, to finish the first draft of *Lincoln*, which, since the draft was the length of three feature-film scripts, required an additional year of nonstop rewriting to get it into filmable shape. (It took another three years of work before we made the film, but that's another story.) And as the clock ticked, the Guthrie festival drew nigh and no new play had appeared. Joe Dowling's understandable concern condensed into open consternation. There was a title, a story was slowly assembling itself in my head, and I had a notebook full of notes, reassuring to me but not to Joe.

I asked my friend Michael Greif to direct the nonexistent play. He said yes before I'd told him what I knew about the story and the characters, which at that point was not much. Michael assembled his splendid design team, telling costume designer Clint Ramos, lighting designer Kevin Adams and sound designer Ken Travis they'd have to wait till there was a script. But since I felt reasonably confident that the play would mainly transpire in the Marcantonios' brownstone, Michael asked Mark Wendland to start designing the set. And composer Michael J. Friedman, scion of a family with red American roots, began to gather musical ideas for a score.

Then, in 2008, less than a year before the scheduled first rehearsal, with eleven characters having acquired a semblance of substance in my head and notebook, Michael and I cast eleven actors, six of whom—Stephen Spinella, Michael Esper, Michael Potts, Kathleen Chalfant, Linda Emond, and Michael Cristofer—were New York actors I'd either worked with or whose work I knew well. The remaining five cast members were from Minneapolis. One cast member, Michelle O'Neill, let me use her name as the character she'd be playing.

I've been undecided about whether or not I should relate what happened next. Friends have advised me not to, concerned that the truth about how the play got written will make it seem like damaged goods. I'm reluctant to tell it because I know that in my heart of hearts, I can't help feeling a certain degree of pride that I wrote, and Michael Greif directed, and eleven intrepid, saintly actors performed in, and the designers designed, and poor Joe Dowling and the magnificent Guthrie Theater administrators and crew produced a splendid production of a four-act, eleven-character play of three hours and forty-five minutes running length that was written in its entirety during its six-week rehearsal period.

I always warn people that I'm a slow writer, and what I really mean by that is I'm a master at delaying for months or years the moment when I have to sit down and write. My saving grace, such as it is, is that eventually my crippling doubts about myself and my work will be overwhelmed by the reality that, if I write nothing, the consequences will be even more disastrous than if I write something terrible. Once I start writing, I'm actually rather quick.

I delivered the first scene of the play on the second day of rehearsal. I brought the director and cast the first draft of the last act at the midnight conclusion of the second of our two ten-hour technical rehearsals. I rewrote furiously all the while, and kept rewriting throughout previews and after opening night.

I hope to be believed that I feel much more shame than pride at what I put everyone through. It was unforgivable. And it left me with a play that probably seemed more coherent and complete than it was. I needed to rewrite it, over and over, which I did for three subsequent productions, and for several years after that. I was seeking out important things that I knew the play knew and I didn't, secrets I suspect got plastered up in the first draft's walls, floors, and ceilings, constructed in too little time under too much pressure. It's taken fourteen years to locate what was hidden, extricate it and bring it out, to the extent of my ability to do so, into the light. The version of the play published in this volume is not entirely different from what premiered in 2009 at the Guthrie. But it is significantly changed. *The Intelligent Homosexual's Guide to Capitalism and Socialism with a Key to the Scriptures* has become the play I always meant to write. Or at any rate, I think it now means what I meant to write—as Mike Nichols used to say, it's what I meant.

A few acknowledgments: I've already mentioned Bill DeFazio's *Longshoremen*, which begins with a brilliant introduction by Stanley Aronowitz. Two other books were of great help to me: Gerald Meyer's biography, *Vito Marcantonio: Radical Politician 1902–1954*; and Bettina Apthekker's *Intimate Politics: How I Grew Up Red, Fought for Free Speech, and Became a Feminist Rebel.*

I'm very grateful to Joe Dowling for commissioning the play and for his faith and support during its nerve-wracking coming-forth.

Joyce Ketay, my agent since I started writing in 1984, traveled with me on my first trip to Minneapolis when it was fourteen degrees below zero. She read the play in installments while I was writing it, made smart comments, put out fires, built up ramparts in production, and listened to me keen and vent, which can't be any fun at all. Her infinite patience, endurance and support is a mystery to me for which I have accumulated thirty-eight-years-and-counting worth of gratitude, indebtedness, and love.

My brother, Eric, and my sister, Lesley, read various versions of the play and were unstintingly enthusiastic and supportive.

Without being asked, Scott Rudin sent the Guthrie Theater a huge check to make the production possible; his early enthusiasm for the play was enormously encouraging.

Mandy Mishel Hackett was invaluable as dramaturg, producer, and friend when the play was at The Public Theater.

Michael Greif is a great director, and he assembled the play's first two productions, at the Guthrie and at The Public Theater in New York, with authoritative insight, magnificent artistry, imperturbable calm, inextinguishable enthusiasm, and thoroughly convincing confidence in a successful outcome. Michael and his designers for the first production—Mark Wendland, Clint Ramos, Kevin Adams, and Ken Travis—brought the world of the play into existence before the same could be said of the play itself.

The late, great Michael J. Friedman wrote a magnificent score.

It's impossible to say how much I owe and how much I miss the irreplaceable Jim Houghton, who co-produced *iHo* in New York City as part of my season as a Signature Theatre playwright.

Over the years, the casts of my plays have had to work hard; learning and assimilating rewrites. But I've never put any actors through the successive tidal waves of incessant changes that the first four *iHo* casts had to endure. These brave and brilliant artists are listed up front in the production history. I'm in awe of all of you, indebted to all of you more than I have words to say, abjectly apologetic and gaga with admiration and gratitude, and I love you all, very very much. To my pals Spinella, Emond, Esper, Potts, Cristofer, Chalfant, Freeman, Wehle, Pasquale, Skraastad, Price, Liberatore, Danson, Lovejoy, Margolis, Kestleman, and Grieg: Marry me. Some of you already have.

Tony Taccone and Gregg Ripley-Duggan were for *iHo*, as Tony has been for everything and Gregg for *nearly* everything I've written, champions and life-savers and pals. Michael Boyd asked me some really tough and necessary questions about what I was on about, and he helped me find several significant answers.

Oskar Eustis has read and helped me rewrite everything I've written. Our thirty-eight-years-and-counting conversation about work, play, plays, theater, politics, love, ambition, ethics, history, eternity, and mortality has helped shape my life, and has made me who I am and how I comprehend the world. I count on Oskar to describe to me what I'm struggling to write. He always finds words that unlock doors and open windows, and I love his deep-sea-diving. I love his mind (and the rest of him too). When Oskar talks about it, playwriting matters. No one has a deeper connection to this particular play than Oskar.

Nor has anyone a more personal connection. *iHo* is dedicated to Oskar's mother and step-father, Doris and Erwin Marquitt, CPUSA members, true believers. Doris and Erwin spent half of every year for a couple of decades teaching in East Berlin. They were honorable, self-sacrificing, very brave, and they cared about essential, human things. I admired them, I found them utterly fascinating, not least because of the many ways in which their complicated lives, especially Doris's, contributed to her son Oskar's unfailingly broad, bracing perspective.

Days before the first preview at the Guthrie, I called my friend and dramaturg, Antonia Grilikhes-Lasky, who lives in New York. She flew to Minneapolis to help me maintain sanity and to fix the script. We took walks along the Mississippi, Antonia listening and questioning as I kvetched and babbled and agonized about what I'd created. Antonia's a highly insightful, analytical reader, and she has a very rare talent for working with writers, at any rate for working with me, defensive, avoidant, querulous, thin-skinned as I am. She's also a wonderful writer—we're currently collaborating on a script— but she's never impatient or imperious, even when I'm slow of wit and/or of pen. She's respectful but insistent when she needs to be, dogged when she knows I've fucked something up. She's very, very smart, and very, very good, and although I've known her for twenty years, I still cannot believe my luck.

As any good husband would do, Mark Harris recalibrated reality for me when the play caused the world to spin off its axis, and he made it possible for me to go to sleep by making it possible for me to believe that what I was trying to do was not absolutely impossible. It was very clever of me, I think, given my penchant for digression and prolixity, to marry a tough, phenomenal editor. Before its second production, Mark convinced me to restructure the second half of the play and he explained how to do it. Mark liked the play's title; I called him after I saw it go by on a poster on the side of a bus in Minneapolis, and he congratulated me for devising "a perfectly grammatical fourteen-word phrase in English guaranteed to give Michele Bachmann a heart attack, and it doesn't even have a verb." (If you don't remember U.S. Representative Bachmann—good! She should be forgotten.) Mark coined *iHo* as the play's diminutive, before which, in conversation, no one knew what to call it.

I'll conclude with a long-overdue expression of the most profound gratitude to my publisher, Terry Nemeth. Terry and I met when I worked at Theatre Communications Group in 1986–1987; I left TCG to write *Angels in America*, which Terry published. His enormous intelligence, decency, patience and indestructible good humor have nurtured me. His passionate conviction that playwrights are serious writers and plays are literature has inspired me. His love of books, verging on the fetishistic, has created a vast, gorgeously clad, exquisitely produced library of contemporary drama that, without Terry Nemeth, simply wouldn't exist.

Terry's retiring this year, in 2022, which would be calamitous for us playwrights, except that Terry's great work is being placed in the awesomely capable, capacious hands of the phenomenal Kathy Sova, who, as editorial director, has painstakingly, lovingly, brilliantly edited TCG's plays, including mine, for twenty-eight years. Kathy and Terry wrangled *iHo* into book form, incorporating rewrites, restructurings, and various typographic experiments. It only took fourteen years. And here it is.

—Tony Kushner
New York City
May 2023

TONY KUSHNER's plays include *A Bright Room Called Day*; *Angels in America, Parts One and Two*; *Slavs!*; *Homebody/Kabul*; the musical *Caroline, or Change*; and the opera *A Blizzard on Marblehead Neck*, both with composer Jeanine Tesori. He has adapted Pierre Corneille's *The Illusion*, S. Y. Ansky's *The Dybbuk*, Bertolt Brecht's *The Good Person of Szechuan* and *Mother Courage and Her Children*, and the English-language libretto for the opera *Brundibár* by Hans Krasa. He wrote the screenplay for Mike Nichols's film of *Angels in America*, and the screenplays for Steven Spielberg's *Munich*, *Lincoln*, *West Side Story*, and *The Fabelmans*, the last of which was co-written with Mr. Spielberg. Mr. Kushner's books include *Brundibar*, with illustrations by Maurice Sendak; *The Art of Maurice Sendak, 1980 to the Present*; and *Wrestling with Zion: Progressive Jewish-American Responses to the Palestinian/Israeli Conflict*, co-edited with Alisa Solomon. Among other honors, Mr. Kushner was awarded a National Medal of Arts by President Barack Obama. He lives in Manhattan with his husband, Mark Harris.

For their generous support of this publication,
Theatre Communications Group would like to offer our
special thanks to: Victoria Abrash and Bruce Allardice;
Susan V. Booth and Max Leventhal; Adrian Budhu;
Carla Ching; Kristen Coury; Joshua Dachs,
Fisher Dachs Associates; Teresa Eyring;
José González y Salazar; Denis Griesmer;
Dwayne Hartford; Michelle Hensley; Susan Hilferty;
Shawn D. Ingram; Marshall Jones III; Lisa Portes;
Meghan Pressman; Francine Thomas Reynolds;
Ellen Richard; Blake Robison; and Elizabeth Rounsavall.

THEATRE COMMUNICATIONS GROUP's mission is to lead for a just and thriving theatre ecology. Through its Core Values of Activism, Artistry, Diversity, and Global Citizenship, TCG advances a better world for theatre and a better world because of theatre. TCG Books is the largest independent trade publisher of dramatic literature in North America, with twenty Pulitzer Prizes for Drama on its book list. The book program commits to the lifelong career of its playwrights, keeping all of their plays in print. TCG Books' authors include: Annie Baker, Nilo Cruz, Jackie Sibblies Drury, Larissa FastHorse, Athol Fugard, Aleshea Harris, Jeremy O. Harris, Quiara Alegría Hudes, David Henry Hwang, Michael R. Jackson, Branden Jacobs-Jenkins, Adrienne Kennedy, The Kilroys, Tony Kushner, Young Jean Lee, Tracy Letts, Martyna Majok, Dominique Morisseau, Lynn Nottage, Dael Orlandersmith, Suzan-Lori Parks, Sarah Ruhl, Stephen Sondheim, Paula Vogel, Anne Washburn, and August Wilson.

Support TCG's work in the theatre field by becoming a member or donor: www.tcg.org

tcg